Kathy and Stella Solve a Murder!

Book and Lyrics by Jon Brittain

Music and Lyrics by Matthew Floyd Jones

methuen | drama

LONDON • NEW YORK • OXFORD • NEW DELHI • SYDNEY

METHUEN DRAMA
Bloomsbury Publishing Plc
50 Bedford Square, London, WC1B 3DP, UK
1385 Broadway, New York, NY 10018, USA
29 Earlsfort Terrace, Dublin 2, Ireland

BLOOMSBURY, METHUEN DRAMA and the Methuen
Drama logo are trademarks of Bloomsbury Publishing Plc

First published in Great Britain 2024

Cover design by Feast Creative

A catalogue record for this book is available from the British Library.

A catalog record for this book is available from the Library of Congress.

ISBN: PB: 978-1-3505-0496-7
ePDF: 978-1-3505-0498-1
eBook: 978-1-3505-0497-4

Series: Modern Plays

Typeset by Mark Heslington Ltd, Scarborough, North Yorkshire
Printed and bound in Great Britain

To find out more about our authors and books visit
www.bloomsbury.com and sign up for our newsletters.

Kathy and Stella Solve a Murder! premiered at the Ambassadors Theatre, London on 25 May 2024, in a production by Francesca Moody Productions, Kater Gordon, Wessex Grove and Fiery Angel. The cast and creative team were as follows:

Kathy Baxter	Bronté Barbé
Stella Carmichael	Rebekah Hinds
Felicia Taylor / Patricia Taylor /	
Horatio Taylor	Hannah-Jane Fox
Justin / Vanessa	Elliot Broadfoot
Slatter	Ben Redfern
Erica / Frankie	Imelda Warren-Green
Detective Inspector Sue Shaw	Elliotte Williams-N'Dure
Understudy Kathy, Stella, Felicia,	
Sue & Erica	Jennifer Caldwell
Understudy Kathy, Stella, Erica,	
Slatter & Justin	Chelsea Hall
Standby Felicia Taylor and	
Sue Shaw	Sorelle Marsh

Band

Keys #1	Andrew Hilton
Keys #2	Catherine Benson
Guitar	Laura Browne
Drums	Philip Williams

Creative Team

Book & Lyrics / Co-Director	Jon Brittain
Music & Lyrics / Arrangements	Matthew Floyd Jones
Co-Director & Choreographer	Fabian Aloise
Set & Costume Designer	Cecilia Carey
Co-Sound Designer	Tingying Dong
Co-Sound Designer	Dan Samson
Lighting Designer	Peter Small
Musical Supervisor and Orchestrator /	
Additional Arrangements	Charlie Ingles
Musical Director	Andrew Hilton
Associate Director	Charlie Martin
Associate Costume Designer &	
Costume Supervisor	Isobel Pellow
Associate Musical Director	Catherine Benson
Props Supervisor	Charlotte King
Hair and Makeup Supervisor	Tevae Humphrey

Music Associate	Tom Mitchell
Dramaturge	Gillian Greer
Casting Director	Annelie Powell CDG
Casting Assistant	Alice Walters
Resident Director	Jennifer Caldwell
Dance Captain	Chelsea Hall
General Manager	Rich Jones
	& Francesca Moody
Production Assistant	Riona Kelly
Production Manager	Titch Gosling
Company Stage Manager	Michael Dennis
Deputy Stage Manager	Caoimhe Regan
Technical Assistant Stage Manager	David Purdie-Smith
Assistant Stage Manager / Book Cover	Phoebe Smyth
Sound No. 1	Karen Szameit
Sound No. 2	Harvey Saunders-Woolley
Head of Wardrobe	Jade Berg
Crew/Flymen	Iain Gonoude
	Joshua Hornsey
	Paul Leslie
	Ben Perkins
Follow Spot Operators	Abigail Grimes
	Megan Taylor

It was first performed at the Paines Plough Roundabout at the Edinburgh Festival Fringe 2022. The original cast was as follows:

Kathy Baxter	Brontë Barbé
Stella Carmichael	Rebekah Hinds
Felicia Taylor / Patricia Taylor /	
Horatio Taylor /	Jodie Jacobs
Detective Inspector Sue Shaw	
Justin / Vanessa / Slatter	TJ Lloyd
Erica / Frankie	Imelda Warren-Green

In 2023, it toured to the Udderbelly at the Edinburgh Festival Fringe, Bristol Old Vic and Manchester Home. The cast was as above and also included:

Ensemble	Jacob Kohli
Ensemble	Sarah Pearson
Off Stage Swing	Chelsea Hall

Acknowledgements

As ever, it takes a village to help bring something to life that never existed before. We are indebted to the following people and massively apologetic to anyone we've missed out:

Francesca Moody, who commissioned the show off a seven minute demo and made all of this happen. Gill Greer, for her dramaturgical brilliance and for Felicia Taylor's severed head. Fabian Aloise, who has done more for the show and us than we could ever sum up — but not least for inventing chaireography. Charlie Ingles, who doesn't know the meaning of 'working hours'. Rich Jones, who made all the books balance without stifling any ambition. Titch Gosling, who juggled egos, fly bars and fake corpses. Bronté Barbé and Rebekah Hinds, who stuck with this random fringe show even when we made them perform it in various tents. Imelda Warren-Green, our secret weapon. Jodie Jacobs, for making us believe our material was legitimately good. TJ Lloyd, for always striking just the right tone. Chelsea Hall, Jacob Kohli and Sarah Pearson, for helping us see what the show could be. Sophie Clay, Anna Mitchelson, Helen Reuben, Teleri Hughes, Elizabeth Ayodele, Tom Penn and everyone else who workshopped the material. Hannah-Jane Fox, Elliot Broadfoot, Elliotte Williams-N'Dure, Ben Redfern, Sorelle Marsh and Jennifer Caldwell, who joined us for this next adventure and have breathed new life into the story. Not to mention all our team members past and present: Cecilia Carey and Peter Small (Team Baby Reindeer), Tingying Dong, Dan Samson, Charlie Martin, Beth Gupwell, Tom Mulliner, Tom Davis, Charlotte King, Isobel Pellow, Tevae Humphrey, Jade Berg, Anna Dixon, Andrew Hilton, Catherine Benson, Philip Williams, Laura Browne, Caitlin Morgan, Tom Mitchell, Ed Borgnis, Caoimhe Regan, Rosie Bannister, Michael Dennis, David Purdie-Smith, Phoebe Smyth, Karen Szameit, Ari Levy, Harvey Saunders-Woolley, Annelie Powell, Alice Walters, Grace Dixon, Elly Roberts, Kieran Lucas, Paul Harfield, Inga Davis-Rutter, Vikki Chandler, Kater Gordon, Ed Snape and Marilyn Eardley, Riona Kelly, Harriet Bolwell and many many more.

Beyond our immediate team, shout outs to: Tasha Dhanraj, for being on the original poster and contributing some of the best jokes. Laura Riddeck, for being our harshest critic ('You're rhyming one with one?!'). Alex Mitchell and Silent Uproar for supporting us early on. Tim Johanson, Mark Cartwright and Lotte Wakeham for bringing us together in the first place. Adam Brace, David Byrne, Phoebe Eclair-Powell, Jamie Hewitt, Richard Marsh, Rich Naylor, Deirdre O'Halloran, Vinay Patel, Matt Tedford, Joe Wilde and all of Jon's friends who read, encouraged and critiqued – he may not have listened to all the notes, but he appreciated them. Everyone at Paines Plough, Underbelly, Bristol Old Vic, Manchester Home and the Ambassadors Theatre. Lily Williams, Mark Starling and Caoimhe Blair for being the best damn agents in the world (in Jon's opinion). And Helen Mumby, Michael Finkle and TJ Wilson for being the best damn agents in the world (in Matthew's opinion).

Finally, a massive thank you to everyone in the Murder Gang who has championed the show over the last four years – but particularly Abbie and Hayley, for creating the fan account, spreading the word, and being part of our story.

See you next murder . . .

Jon Brittain & Matthew Floyd Jones – May '24

Kathy and Stella Solve a Murder!

For a girl not *named Fran – the onewhoactuallydunnit*

> *. . . and also Dot and Rox from the Channel 4*
> *reality show* Murder Island.

They walked in evidence so that Kathy and Stella might run.

Notes

Kathy and Stella Solve a Murder! *is a musical (hence the exclamation mark).*

Our production of the show is performed by a cast of seven – with lots of doubling. But it doesn't have to be – there can be as many people as there are parts.

The story takes place over multiple locations but the action is largely continuous – it's jump cuts rather than lengthy scene changes.

Lyrics are indented and we've tried to represent them as accurately as possible – but we've excluded some of the less relevant backing vocals.

Sometimes we've added letters into a word to show when people are holding a note for a long time when siiiiiingiiiiing.

*For brevity, when Kathy and Stella speak or sing together, we have sometimes used '****Both****' as the character heading. We don't use it for any other pairings.*

(. . .) an ellipsis means a thought trails off or is not completed.

(/) a slash indicates overlapping dialogue.

(–) a dash at the end of the line means a thought has been interrupted.

(-) a hyphen between two words is where a comma didn't feel exciting enough.

(=) an equals sign before character names means that the lyrics in question are sung simultaneously.

(V/O) means voiceover.

This text went to print before the show opened. It was accurate at the time of submission but Jon is hugely indecisive and so the actual show will probably have changed multiple times by the time you read this – whatcanyado!

Act One

We're in a garage. Full of clutter and knickknacks. The band is hidden in the eaves. A corkboard hangs on the garage door with various cuttings pinned onto it connected by red string (in classic detective/ conspiracy theorist style). We'll travel to a lot of different places in the next two hours – but they will all emerge out of this one location.

As the audience comes in they are treated to a fun musical Megamix of the tunes from the show in the style of 00s indie rock – the sort **Kathy** *and* **Stella** *might have been fans of as teenagers.*

Gradually, a new sound fades in – a brief overture, layered with historic news reports about a horrific murder. It builds to a peak until . . . Boom – thunder and lightning – and we're off!

The underscore for 'The Prologue' begins. It's spooky, atmospheric, intense – trying too hard to be cool, like a student production of 'Jesus Christ Superstar'.

A mysterious figure enters – we'll know him later as **Horatio Taylor** *– but for now, he acts as a Blood Brothers-esque narrator. A* **Chorus** *of newspaper-reading Hull residents slowly enter to accompany him.*

Horatio
> The murder spree started without warning
> As murder sprees . . . tend to do
> But slowly the truth started dawning
> That the killings were connected
> *And there's a psycho on the loose!*

Chorus
> A psycho's on the loose

Horatio
> He started out in Humberside
> But soon the legend spread
> He had a deadly calling card
> He chopped off people's heads

Don't know who I'm talking about then let me educate ya
All about the man they called . . .

THE HULL DECAPITATOR

Chorus
Decapitator Decapitator Decapitator

Horatio
His crimes they were horrendous

Chorus
He left no clues, he left no trace

Horatio
The investigation endless

Chorus
Will no one ever crack the case?

Horatio
His reign of terror lasted years
Collecting heads as souvenirs
'Til the day the killings stopped

Chorus
The day he disappeared

Horatio
And though this happened years ago
He's still out there for all we know . . .

Horatio *and* **Chorus**
Oh was this case just meant to be consigned to history?
Would this man's identity remain a mystery?

They all begin singing over each other in an epic canon.

Who could ever solve . . .?
Who could ever solve it . . .?
Who could ever solve a crime . . .?
Who could ever solve a crime like this . . .?

As this climaxes, the **Chorus** *disperse and the intensity of the first song gives way to the indomitably perky refrain of 'Kathy and Stella's Murder Podcast' . . .*

A single microphone and a laptop are set up to record.

Our heroes **Kathy** *and* **Stella** *enter in wheelie chairs, ready to begin their latest episode.*

Kathy
Hello people

Stella
All you lovely listeners

Both
Thanks for joining us again!

Stella
Welcome back

Kathy
If you're new here

Stella
You've stumbled on our podcast

Kathy
Or it's been recommended by a friend

Both
Just sit back and relax

Kathy
We're coming to you from my mum's garage

Stella
With crackers and cheese and a bottle of Pinot on the side

Both
Our show has been described as the perfect marriage

Kathy
Of boozy jokes

Stella
Cheeky banter

Both
    And in depth chat about homicide!

Stella   That's right, listeners – we're going to be telling you all about our *favourite* murders.

Kathy   Only not using that word!

Stella   What, murders?

Kathy   No, favourite! We're not ranking them.

Stella   Yeah, obviously . . . but if we had pick a top five – *we could*!

Both
    The show's about true crime
    We're obsessed with murder
    If it's sick, perverse or twisted
    You know that we just can't resist it
    We've done the reading
    All the facts and figures
    We've plumbed the depths of Wikipedia
    To research every vile misdeed for ya
    Decapitation and sex cult mass-suicide

Stella
    Stabbing

Kathy
    Shooting

Stella
    Hanging

Kathy
    Drowning

Both
    Poisoning with cyanide
    Strangulation then gouging out the eyes
    Psycho rapist cannibals who burn their victims ALIVE
    And yes . . .

Kathy
If you're suffering with trauma

Both
These tales may cause distress

Stella
Turn off, it's not for you

Both
But still nevertheless
Consider this your trigger warning
From this point on there's no turning back
No deviations we're staying on track
The show that you're listening to
Is . . .
Kathy and Stella's Murder Podcast
We've got crimes for you
Kathy and Stella's Murder Podcast
Every single one is true!
The murder podcast with Kathy and Stella
Don't turn off we've got lots to tell ya
Join us now 'cause we're having a blast
On Kathy and Stella's Murder Podcast

Vanessa, **Kathy**'s *mum, enters with a full washing up basket.*

Vanessa   Kathryn, sweetheart, are you nearly done in
there? I need to put a wash on.

Kathy   Not now, Mum! We're just recording an episode.

Vanessa   Well, don't be too long. Your dad'll need
somewhere to park the car . . .

Vanessa *exits.*

Kathy   But in case you haven't heard us before . . .

My name's Kathy

Stella
And I'm Stella

Kathy
I work in a library

Stella
I'm between jobs

Kathy
We're from Beverley – near Hull

Both
You won't have heard of it

Stella
She's my best friend

Kathy
And she's mine

Stella
We went to school together

Kathy
Since Year 5

Stella
She's the person that I call

Both
When things turn to shit

Kathy
We've always been a little bit obsessed with murder

Stella
Not just the famous ones that everybody's heard of

Kathy
And though it's true our audience is small

Stella   So far!

Both
One day we'll show the world the best true crime podcast
of them all is . . .
Kathy and Stella's Murder Podcast

But hey – by now you've probably got that
So let's read out some . . .

The song suddenly transitions into a dad rock-style jingle. Other cast members become the show's **Listeners**, *singing along.*

Kathy, Stella *and* **Listeners**
LISTENER EMAILS!
LISTENER EMAILS!
Give us your feedback
We love to receive mail!

Different **Listeners** *step forward in turn – singing their messages.*

Kathy   First up . . .

Ruthless92 says

Ruthless92
OMG I love you – you are everything!

Stella   Aw, right back at ya, mate.

Kathy   ForensicSteve says

ForensicSteve
ACTUALLY I think you'll find

Stella   Yeah, blah blah blah – we made a mistake!

Kathy   Disrespectress says

Disrespectress
You should be ashamed
Using people's pain for your enter-

Stella
Yeah, we know!

Kathy
And Doomscroller's sent us seven DMs
Saying

Doomscroller
EAT COCK AND DIE YOU FUCKING LESBIANS

Beat.

Stella   . . . so that's nice!

The **Chorus** *kicks back in.*

Both
  Kathy and Stella's murder podcast
  Accept no substitute
  Kathy and Stella's murder podcast
  The perfect length for your commute
  Your A to Z with Kathy and Stella
  Documenting every serial killer
  Tales to shock and flabbergast
  Well researched and unbiased
  Hit subscribe and do it fast!
  To Kathy and Stella's
  Murrrrrrder Podcaaaaaast
  Podcast
  Podcast
  Kathy and Stella's Murder Podcast

The song finishes and we segue to the end of their episode.

Kathy   And so, dear listeners, that concludes the case of the
Sedgefield Shoelace Strangler.

Stella   In conclusion, not a great guy.

Kathy   But in some ways misunderstood and a victim
himself.

Stella   What? No he wasn't! He literally strangled people
with shoelaces!

Kathy   Yeah . . . but only as a cry for help.

Stella   *Anyway* – we've gotta sign off now, murder gang
– we've got a very *exciting* meeting to go to!

Kathy   Erm! Which we said we weren't going to talk about!

Stella   IT'S ONLY WITH FELICIA BLOODY TAYLOR!

Kathy   *Stella!*

Stella   What? We can edit that out. That's right murder gang, THE Felicia Taylor is here in Hull for a book signing. Our favourite true crime author of all time AND the woman who solved the case of the *Hull Decapitator*.

Kathy   Fact check! That's never actually been accepted by the authorities.

Stella   Yeah, but only 'cause he killed himself before he could stand trial! That's right – I'm talking about local burger van owner and notorious weirdo . . .

Both   *Billy Fingers!*

Stella   Who, twenty years ago, Felicia Taylor identified as the culprit in her landmark book about the case – 'Heads Will Roll'.

Kathy   See episode one in our iTunes.

Stella   And now she's about to launch her very own True Crime Podcast Network – which, without saying too much, is *absolutely looking for new shows*! So, we've gotta go now, murder gang.

Kathy   But until next time . . .

A short jingle accompanies their sign off.

Both
   See you next murder!

They stop recording. As they begin to get ready, an underscore for 'We're Gonna Wow Felicia Taylor' begins, pulsing with excitement.

Stella   Right, I've got listener figures, finances, our five year plan, and a mood board with evocative imagery to show her what our vibe is. Mainly murder. Do you know what you're going to say about the show?

Kathy   Yeah, that's it's a kind of exploration of the crippling anxiety women feel because of our vulnerability in a patriarchal world designed to enable and encourage the violent crimes of men. But funny.

Stella   She's gonna bloody love it!

Kathy   Yeah, I dunno, but what if . . .

Stella   I know – what if the show becomes a global sensation and the sheer enormity of its success gets in the way of our friendship? Kathy, I don't care how successful we become across multiple mediums – you and me come first.

Kathy   I was gonna say . . . What if she doesn't like it?

Stella   Er – none of that please! That's impossible.

You and me, we've shared so much
Since the day we met in that sandpit

Kathy
Friendship bracelets

Stella
Our emo phase

Both
And Buffy the Vampire Slayer fanfic!
The bond we have is special we
Will outshine all the rest

Stella
You'll see – it's true
And what'll make it even better

Kathy
Is that we're doing it together

Both
Our hobby
Soon will be our full time job – because
We're gonna wow Felicia Taylor
She's gonna love our show for sure

Stella
I laid the groundwork with my email

Kathy
You've given her the gist

Stella
That's right!
So how could she resist?
C'mon

Both
It's time to wow Felicia Taylor
She's gonna make our
True crime dreams come true

Stella
She's gonna make our show a massive hit!

Kathy
We'll get some sponsors and monetise it!

Both
That's the plan and there's no room for failure
C'mon let's go and wow Felicia Taylor

As **Stella** *leaves,* **Kathy**'s *mum,* **Vanessa**, *enters again – anxious, tentative, but persistent.*

Vanessa   Ah, Kathryn, sweetheart.

Kathy   Mum! Hi – I was just off out –

Vanessa   With Stella, yes. I was just wondering if you'd looked at the application form I gave you – for the teacher training course.

Elsewhere, **Stella**'s *sister enters –* **Frankie**, *tough, stressed out, perpetually let down. The two scenes play out in parallel.*

Frankie   Where do you think you're going? You said you'd do a shift for me in the bar! And you owe me rent!

Stella   What – no I didn't! And can't you get someone who's not your sister? I've got a thing.

Kathy   I've got to go!

Vanessa
Darling, I don't want to criticise

Frankie
Of course! You're letting me down again!

Frankie *and* **Vanessa**
Don't you think there's more to life
Than a murder podcast with your silly friend?

Vanessa
You've got to put yourself out there

Frankie
You could at least pretend to care

Frankie *and* **Vanessa**
I know that you're not doing this to hurt me
But you're broke and pushing thirty

Vanessa   I know when you moved back home you needed time to work on your anxiety, but that was almost eight years ago. You can't volunteer in a library forever.

Frankie   Ever since Mum died I've supported you. And for what? You've got no job, no savings, you're living on my sofa! When are you going to grow up?

Vanessa
Think of all the skills you've got to share

Frankie
Just get an actual job!

Vanessa
Like netball or grade five piano or your silver Duke of Edinburgh

Frankie
Can you just try being responsible
You're not the only one who wants it all

Vanessa   Please . . .

You were meant for so much more than this

Frankie

I'm not taking any more of this

Vanessa

You've got to stop ignoring this

Frankie

And y'know what?

Both

From now on . . . I'm not supporting this!

They exit – leaving **Kathy** *and* **Stella***'s confidence shaken – the two friends reapproach each other, panicked.*

Both

We need to wow Felicia Taylor
Everything is on the line

Kathy

It's too much!

Stella

I need to bail!

Both

No, you can't just run and hide

Kathy

Arghh, I've broken out in hives

Both

Oh shit!
How can we wow Felicia Taylor?
Next to her, we may's well not exist!
No!
You've got to do it for your friend, she needs you
Grit your teeth, you can succeed
C'mon, just take a breath on your inhaler

They each take a breath on their inhalers.

Then go out there and wow Felicia Taylor

The song becomes more sweeping and dreamy.

'Cause once we have then nothing stands between us
And living the kind of life we've always dreamed of

Kathy
I'll be free from anxiety

Stella
I won't be such a liability

Both
'Cause once Felicia's made us true crime famous
From that day on, no one will mock or shame us

Kathy
We'll have listeners galore

Stella
Every week a million more

Both
An ending happier than any fairy tale – and

Kathy
To bring to life the fantasy we share

Stella
Find your inner queen and unleash her

Both
That's the way we'll wow Feliiiiicia . . .
Tayloooor

A bunch of **True Crime Fans** *arrive as* **Kathy** *and* **Stella** *get to the signing.*

True Crime Fans
Got to wow Felicia Taylor
Need to wow Felicia Taylor
Oh my God – Felicia Taylor

Both
Wow Felicia Taylor!

Felicia Taylor *makes her grand entrance onstage – high status, glam, doesn't give a fuck. She has a copy of her book 'Heads Will Roll'.*

Felicia   And so . . .

That's how I finally cracked the case
Of the Hull Decapitator
But, darlings – once upon a time I was just like all of you
My life was plain and dull
So remember – keep on dreaming . . . Hull!

And one day you might solve a true crime too . . .

Applause and camera flashes as the appearance ends. A fruity jazz bass line begins for 'True Crime Famous'.

That's my time! I'll see you all outside for photos and autographs! Bye bye now, bye bye!

She gets offstage. Her adoring **Fans** *flock to her –* **Kathy** *and* **Stella** *push to the front.*

Stella   Ms. Taylor – over here!

Kathy   Thank you so much for meeting us!

Felicia   I'm sorry . . . who?

Stella   We emailed. About the podcast . . .?

Felicia   Podcast . . .?

She approaches them – the other fans watch the encounter, becoming a chorus for her.

Oh, of course! It's Karen, Cilla!
Are those your names, I can't recall
Never mind, let's get this over with
Oops, just a sec
I've got to take this call

She takes out a phone and answers.

Hi Paul, yes darling, I've seen the front cover, I think we might need a more attractive corpse. Who'd be upset about *her* dying? (*Laughs.*) OK, byeeee!

She hangs up.

Now . . .

> Back to business Kirsty, Sarah
> Soz, I don't know which one's which
> But let's move on, 'cause I haven't got long
> To give you feedback on your pitch . . .
> Saffy and Kelly's Murder Podcast
> So cute, and you both seem nice
> But I think it pays to be realistic
> So let me give you some free advice

She takes centre stage – loving the attention.

> You wanna be
> True crime famous?
> With a hit no one can ignore
> Well, you can't just do
> The same as
> Every other podcast that's come before
> Y'know, the market place is crowded
> So unless my judgement's clouded
> I'd say you need to go right back to the drawing board
> 'Cause frankly, girls, I'm bored.

She walks away from them – they pursue, pushing through the fans to get to her.

Stella   What? No, wait!

Kathy
> Please, Miss Taylor

Stella
> It's not just a podcast . . .

Kathy
> No, we also read out . . . emails . . .?

Both
    And sometimes . . . there's . . . a quiz?

Felicia   A quiz?! You never mentioned a quiz!!! Oh my god!
In that case . . . I still don't care. Listen, girls . . .

    You wanna wow Felicia Taylor
    I'm gonna need a little more – we
    Can't just bore them with bland narration
    We need to be part of the story

She gestures for them to step back.

Give me space!

A hard spotlight on her – she goes full indulgent diva.

    Look at me, my reputation
    Comes from solving the Hull Decapitations
    I know this may be stressful
    But frankly, girls, you're nothing special
    Until you find your very own USP . . .

(*Clarifying.*) Unique selling point.

    Well, it's a *no* from meeee.

As she holds this last note, the fans circle her singing.

True Crime Fans
    True crime famous
    True crime famous
    True crime famous

They all pose for the button.

Felicia   It's a no from me!

Felicia *and her fans leave –* **Kathy** *and* **Stella** *are left alone,
downhearted.*

Stella   Not special? *Not special?!* She can take her 'not
special' and shove it up her arse!

Kathy   Stella –

Stella   I should have prepared. If I'd said the right thing. Stupid stupid stupid!

Kathy   No, you heard her. She just . . . didn't like it.

Stella   Yeah – 'cause I'm a massive fuck up.

Kathy   You're not the fuck up. If anyone's a fuck up, I'm the fuck up.

Stella   Mate, you're fucked up if you think you're a fuck up.

Kathy   Well. Then, so are you.

They share a moment. Tender music begins. A ballad – 'If I Didn't Have You (I Would Die)'.

Y'know before we started doing this, I didn't have anything. You gave me something to live for. I don't care if she didn't like it. There's only one person whose opinion matters to me.

Stella   Greta Thunberg?

Kathy   No, you.

Kathy
   I used to think there was no one like me till the day that I met you

Stella
   I hated pretty much everyone till I found someone who hated everyone too

Both
   Other friends may share a bond

Kathy
   But no one else

Stella
   No, no one else

Both
   Compares . . . to us

Kathy

'Cause I know that not a single one of them

Stella

Has found someone who's

Both

So the one for them

Kathy

And
If I didn't have you I would die
If I didn't have you I don't know how I . . .
Could even get dressed in the morning
Or do anything at all
No reason to try
'Cause without you I'd die

Stella   Thanks, mate.

If I didn't have you I would also die
If I didn't have you no other best friends need apply
You're completely irreplaceable
I'm never gonna give you up
Just like Rick Astley
You mean too much to me . . .

Both

Who would I share my stupid thoughts with?
Who would I laugh until I snort with?

Kathy

We're meant to be and that you can't deny

Stella

We're codependent

Both

Oh tell me how would I keep going?
Why would my blood continue flowing?

Kathy

When losing you would make me want to die

They begin to joke with each other, playing up the melodrama of it all – miming various forms of death and murder.

Stella
   If I didn't have you I would die!

Kathy
   No – if I didn't have you I would
   Actually!

Stella
   Genuinely!

Kathy
   Literally!

Both
   Immediately DIE!

Their game climaxes and the song suddenly becomes softer – very sincere.

Kathy
   If I didn't have you I'd be terrified

Stella
   If I didn't have you I'd just run away and hide

Both
   I'd curl up in a little ball
   And disappear from view

Kathy
   That's what I'd do

Stella
   I'd do that too
   And that's why

Kathy
   And that's why

Both
   Without you I would die

Stella   I'll see you tomorrow.

Kathy You'll always see me tomorrow.

They exit as the song ends.

Elsewhere, it's night, dark, **Felicia** *re-enters, on the phone.*

Felicia They said they'd send a car, well, it didn't arrive! No, I do not want to wait in Costa. Have you ever been in one? Well, I haven't and I intend for it to stay that way.

Offstage, the sound of a kicked can.

Finally!

She walks towards it – we hear the following but only see it in silhouette.

Hello? Hello?

A shadowy figure approaches her.

Oh, it's you. No! What are you doing?

The figure draws a large knife and brandishes it above their head.

No, no, get away from me! *I'M A SUCCESSFUL AUTHOR!*

As the knife comes down, the lights cut to red – we hear a blood curdling scream.

A rocking kind of number begins – spiky and exciting – 'Part of the Story'.

It's the next morning. **Kathy** *answers her mobile to* **Stella**.

Stella Oh my God, Kathy, you'll never guess where I am.

Kathy Stella, you'll never guess where I am.

Stella I just got woken up by –

Both The police.

Kathy Me too! They said they want to ask some –

Both Questions.

Stella Same! Then they brought me to –

Both   The police station!

They see each other. Two police officers enter and escort them inside.

Both   Oh for God's sake!

Stella
   OK, stop, what the fuck is happening here?

Officer 1   Please come this way.

Stella
   This is TOO weird

Kathy
   I agree, this is kind of MASSIVELY UNUSUAL

Stella
   Oh my God, what if we've been falsely accused

Officer 2   Just take a seat.

Kathy
   I'm so confused!

Stella
   If you stitch us up I swear, we'll bloody sue you all!

They sit down.

Both
   Are you thinking what I'm thinking
   'Cause I'm thinking that you probably are

Stella   We've been framed, there's a massive conspiracy, it goes all the way to the top – it's like 'Line of Duty', we're in 'Line of Duty'!

Kathy   Yeah . . .

   But it doesn't matter what or why

Stella
   We can be each other's alibi!

Kathy
No – we need to breathe and just stay calm – in
Spite of this being quite alarming!

DI Sue Shaw *enters, authoritative, overworked, and no time for
frivolity.*

Sue   Ms. Baxter, Ms. Carmichael, My name's Detective
Inspector Sue Shaw. Thank you for coming in.

Stella   Don't thank us, pig! What are you gonna do? Arrest
us on trumped up charges and fix us up for something we
haven't done?

Sue   I was *planning* on asking you some questions.

Stella   That's how it starts.

Sue
Did you meet Felicia Taylor last night?

Stella
Don't answer that

Kathy
We did, that's right

Stella
And if one of her books got stolen that's a coincidence
It wasn't me

Sue
That's not the reason we've asked you here

Kathy
Then why?

Sue
This might be hard to hear
But after she left the signing, there was an incident

Kathy *and* **Stella**
Are you saying what we think you're saying . . .?

Sue   Yes. At approximately 10pm last night, Felicia Taylor
was murdered.

This hits **Kathy** *and* **Stella** *hard – we focus in on them as the song becomes more haunted, anxious, ghostly.*

Both
  It's the weirdest feeling in the world
  To have your nightmares realised
  This fear we've had since we were girls
  We're shocked but somehow not surprised

Sue   You were two of the last people to see her.

Both
  That small pervasive thought that's ever growing

Sue   Is there anything you can remember?

Both
  Like we've been waiting for it but not knowing

Sue   Anything at all?

The song begins to build again as they make a shared realisation . . .

Both
  The reality cuts to the core
  But on top of that there's something more
  'Cause her death while terrifying
  Also means that you and I are
  Part of the story
  At the start of the story
  Pinch me now, reassure me
  That we're both not still asleep

Stella *pinches* **Kathy**.

Kathy   Ow!

Both
  We're really
  Part of the story?
  At the heart of a story
  It's scary and a little bit thrilling to be
  Part of the story

They're back in the room – eager to assist.

Kathy
  Of course we'll help – oh God, I feel sick

Stella
  We won't rest till you've caught this prick!

Sue
  OK, did you notice anything peculiar . . .?

The music peters out as they rack their brains . . .

Stella   Erm . . . well, no.

Sue   Any useful information?

Kathy   . . . nothing specific.

Sue   Right. Well, thank you for coming in.

Sue *goes to leave.*

Stella   Wait! You can't leave it there! She was the most famous true crime author in the world – and she's been murdered!

Kathy   And we were her biggest fans!

Stella   Yeah, so we might hold the key to cracking the whole case!

Sue   Oh, yes, sorry, I've been doing this for over twenty-five years and I'm working with a team of qualified detectives but I'll tell you everything in case you have an insight that we've missed, yeah?

Beat.

Now if you'll excuse me, I have to get back to unjustly prosecuting people for things they haven't done.

Sue *goes to leave, then turns back.*

Sorry, I shouldn't joke about that, that is genuinely a problem.

Sue *exits, leaving* **Kathy** *and* **Stella** *alone.*

Stella
   Are you thinking what I think you're thinking?

Kathy
   Yes. I think that I probably am

Both
   Felicia said we need a USP
   It's morbid but ironically
   An investigation into her death'll
   Be the thing that makes us special

Sue *re-enters.*

Sue   *Wait!* You're not planning on trying to solve this yourselves, are you?

Stella   Erm . . .

Kathy   No!

Stella   No.

Kathy   No no no no.

Stella   As if!

Kathy   Definitely not.

Sue   Good. Got enough on my plate without amateurs getting involved.

She leaves.

Beat.

They burst into song again.

Both
   We're gonna be
   Part of the story

Stella
   We're gonna solve it!

Both
    Part of the story!
    Let's get investigatory
    So we can crack this case wide open
    Now we're
    Part of the story
    We are
    Stars of the story

We transition into their garage – the microphone is set up – their
Listeners *dance around them.*

Both
    Test the mic, press record 'cause you and me . . .
    . . . are part of the storyyy

Listeners
    Got to avenge Felicia Taylor's DEATH
    Avenge Felicia Taylor's DEATH
    Avenge Felicia Taylor

Kathy *and* **Stella** *check themselves and become serious again.*

Both
    And of course it's very sad that she's been murdered

The spooky music of the prologue returns – a ghostly **Felicia** *enters*
as **Stella** *reads her book.*

Felicia
    And so the investigation began
    A thrilling chase
    A race against time
    But how long till I found my man
    And solved the case as old as true crime . . .

Stella *closes the book,* **Felicia** *disappears again.*

Stella   Say what you like about her – that bitch could write.

Kathy   Anything useful in there?

Stella   Sweet fuck all, mate. She barely investigated a thing. She got a massive tip-off on page thirteen from her anonymous source.

Both   D.C.S.

Stella   He told her all about Billy Fingers – basically solved the whole crime for her. I wish we had an anonymous source. We don't even have a . . . nonymous one. What about you?

Kathy   Nothing. I went to the crime scene but they've cleared it away. They don't give CCTV footage to civilians. And the woman on the police tip line said it's set up for people to give *them* information, not the other way round.

A new song begins, a frustratingly up-temp bossa nova – 'Fuck! We Don't Know What We're Doing'.

Stella   This is impossible! We've got no motives. No suspects. We don't know anything. Urgh. Who knew solving a murder would be so hard.

Kathy   No. We've just got to stick to the facts.

Stella *rolls her eyes,* **Kathy** *tries to encourage her.*

Kathy   OK.

Let's slow down – and start again from the beginning
I know, it's big but that's OK!
Y'know what they say – hey!
People solve murders every day!

Stella   No one's ever said that.

Kathy   Whatever!

I think that all we need is a system
Gather all the clues and list 'em

Stella

So we haven't missed any

Kathy

Then we'll be methodical – like Sherlock

Stella

Here, I've opened up a Google Word doc!

Kathy   Perfect!

Stella   I'll type.

Kathy

We know she got into town at six that day then
Was killed in a car park near the train station . . .

Beat.

. . . OK, that's all we've got so far
But still that's kind of a start . . .?
And while we've got no forensic experts we can call on

Stella

Or relevant experience we can draw from

Kathy

Or the power to question under caution

Both

Or the faintest clue what we're doing at all – one
Thing we know for sure

Kathy

For sure!

Both

Is with our true crime knowledge and passion it
Can't be long before we're smashing it!

Beat. Their confidence collapses.

FUCK!
We don't know what we're doing here
We haven't got the first idea how to
Turn ourselves into detectives
It's much harder than we both expected

Stella
 We bought a cork board and string and stuff

Kathy
 Yeah, I'm starting to think that might not be enough

Both
 We've only begun but still already we're stuck
 We don't know what we're doing – fuck!

Kathy   Something'll come up – we just have to keep going.

As they sing, the ghost of **Felicia** *enters and re-enacts the scenario they are describing – with a a True Crime Fan named* **Fran**.

Kathy
 Hey, look!
 ForensicSteve just sent us a photo
 Of Felicia and a true crime fan

Fran
 A girl named Fran

Fran *takes a selfie of her and* **Felicia**.

Kathy
 And – she posted this a week ago on Instagram

Stella
 And?

Kathy
 Look in the background behind them!

Stella *gasps*.

Both
 That's the Primark in Hull!

Stella   What?

Kathy
 She was here a week before we thought she was!

Stella

    Hey – and that's not all!

    Ruthless92's sent us the website – for Felicia's publisher in Spain!

The ghost of **Felicia** *takes out a flamenco-style fan and is joined by a chorus of Spanish dancers as the song takes on a Latin vibe.*

Stella

    They've accidentally pre-announced her new book – and this is it's name

Felicia

    'El proyecto de crimen real secreto de Felicia Taylor'

Stella

    Let me just run that through an online translator . . .

Chorus

    'Felicia Taylor's Secret True Crime Project'

Both   What can it mean?

Chorus

    'Felicia Taylor's Secret True Crime Project'

Beat. Again, they haven't a clue.

Both   *Uuuggggh!!!*

    FUCK!
    We don't know what we're doing here
    Everything is so unclear
    Oh, the clues are there but we just can't detect them
    When we do then we just can't connect them

Kathy

    We've got no training or technique

Stella

    It's much harder than it looks on Jonathan Creek

Both
> We need a break-through now before it's too late
> But we don't know what we're doing . . .

Kathy
> Wait!

The ghost of **Felicia** *enters, this time benign.*

Kathy
> What would Felicia do?
> If she were solving this with me and you

Stella
> She'd say

Felicia
> Utilise all your resources

Stella
> And we've got the internet!

Both
> Let's open source this!

Stella   What do you think X – formerly known as Twitter?

The chorus become **Tweeters**, *spewing out conspiracy theories.*

Tweeter 1
> Could be a satanist cult!

Tweeter 2
> Or the Illuminati!

Tweeter 3
> Or a rival author!

Tweeter 4
> It was Neo-Nazis!

Tweeter 5
> Y'know the Queen is a lizard!

Tweeter 6
It could be an owl!

Doomscroller *emerges from the* **Tweeters**.

Doomscroller
Eat cock and die you fucking lesbians!

Both
FUCK!
We don't know what we doing here

Tweeters
It could be Nazis!

Both
We're trying our best to persevere

Tweeters
Illuminati!

Both
We're actually getting really lost here
Starting to feel like we're imposters

Kathy
Can someone tell us what to do

Stella
'Cause basically we don't have a clue

Both
We thought we'd be naturals but it's starting to look like
we suck!

Tweeters
They suck!

Both
'Cause we don't know what we're doing!

Tweeters
They don't know what they're doing

Both
   We don't know what we're doing!

Tweeters
   They don't know what they're doing!

A package is handed to **Stella**.

Stella   We just got a package.

Kathy   What is it?

Stella   It's . . .

Stella *takes out a clear plastic bag containing* **Felicia Taylor**'s *bloodied severed head.*

Both   FELICIA TAYLOR'S SEVERED HEAD IN A BAG!

They are both horrified.

Tweeters
   They don't know what they're doing

Kathy *and* **Stella**
   FUCK!

As the song ends **Stella** *drops the head – it hits the ground with a thud . . .*

. . . and **Sue** *enters again, we are now in a hospital.*

Sue   *Step away from the head.* That is evidence in an ongoing homicide investigation. Why did someone send it to you?

Kathy   We already told you – we don't know!

Stella   Maybe they listen to the show?

Sue   Oh yes, the show you told me you weren't going to do.

Stella   Yeah, well, you never told us she had her head chopped off!

Kathy   A massive link to the Hull Decapitator.

A constable wearing rubber gloves picks up the head and takes it away.

Sue   Yes, believe it or not, I did notice that. That's *why* I don't want you involved. If this is a copycat killer, they're doing it for *attention*. Now, if you breathe a word of this to anybody . . . I can't arrest you, but I will be very angry.

Sue *leaves.*

Stella   She could have said thank you. We brought it all the way here. Now I've got to clean blood, hair and bloody hair out of my sister's car before she gets home! What do we do now?

Kathy   You heard her, there's nothing we can do. At least we found a clue. No one can take that away from us . . . Except when she did just then.

Justin, *a nice young man who works in the morgue, approaches.*

Justin   Sorry, I just . . . is it Kathy Baxter and Stella Carmichael? Oh my God! It's Justin Norris – from school! We were in home economics together!

Stella   Oh wow! Justin Norris! (*To* **Kathy**.) He fancied you!

Kathy (*mortified*)   What? No! Stella! He didn't! You didn't! I know you didn't. You didn't, did you . . . did you? No, I know you didn't. Just ignore her, she's being . . . Sorry, what are you doing here?

Justin   I'm a morgue technician. I know, look how far I've come in the world! And I listen to your show!

Stella   You listen to the podcast?

Justin
      KATHY AND STELLA'S MURDER PODCAST!

I download it every week. Me and my colleague Erica put it on as we clean up after post-mortems. Erica! Look who it is!

Erica *approaches – innocent, enthusiastic, VERY EXCITED.*

Erica   Oh my God.

A quirky refrain begins, as she sings a little too intensely.

I really can't believe it – total fangirl moment!
You're actually here – you're my actual heroes!
I love the show, I love you two, I love everything you do!
Your podcast makes me feel like someone actually cares
I tell all my friends about you
They're like please shut up about you
I'm your biggest fan, it's like you live in my ears!

Beat.

Stella   Thanks . . .

Kathy   Yeah, thank you.

Stella   I think?

Justin   Hey, look, technically I could get fired for doing this but . . . do either of you fancy a tour of the morgue . . .?

Stella   No thanks, mate – I think we've had enough blood and brains for one day.

Kathy (*impulsively*)   Actually, I'd quite like to. If that's OK?

Beat. A tiny moment of tension. **Stella** *wasn't expecting that.*

Stella   Sure. I'll just stay out here and *not* tell our biggest fan about that time the murderer sent us Felicia Taylor's severed head!

Erica   Oh my God, what?

Stella   Let me tell you all about it.

Stella *takes* **Erica** *by the arm, leading her away to tell all . . .*

. . . as we follow **Kathy** *and* **Justin** *down to the morgue.*

Justin   I can't believe I'm with Kathy Baxter! I remember you at school – you were always SO clever with your poems and stories and stuff. I thought you were gonna go off to Oxford or Harvard and become Prime Minister or Susie Dent on Countdown.

Kathy   Well, I got as far as Reading. I wasn't really cut out for English literature . . . or university . . . or people . . . basically I didn't leave my room for three months and then I had an emotional breakdown in a Co-op.

Justin   . . . but now you work in a library. That's exciting.

Kathy   Not really. It's mostly asking old men not to use the computers to look at pornography. Otherwise, it's pretty dead.

Justin   Not as dead as in here. On which note . . . TA DA!

A Disney-like twinkling begins to play – like the Little Mermaid in her cave of treasures. **Kathy** *stares open mouthed . . .*

Kathy
Oh my God . . . It's AMAZING
The autopsy table, the refrigerated chambers
The organ scales!
It's all just like I imagined it would be

A Motown like riff begins – fast retro soul – 'Never Felt So Alive'.

Justin   Looks like you should be giving me the tour.

Kathy   Oh, yeah, sorry . . .

It's just – I've always been a little obsessed with death

Justin
Don't worry – so was I!

Kathy
When all the other kids were watching Disney

Justin
Let me guess? You were watching CSI

Kathy
Never interested in ballet or horses

Justin
You were playing

Kathy *and* **Justin**
Doctors and corpses

Kathy
People around me all thought I was broken

Justin
They don't understand

Kathy *and* **Justin**
This is just a way of coping

Kathy
With the stress and the pressure

Justin
Regrets and depression

Kathy
Distress at rejection
And deceptive perceptions
Did I say my obsessiveness . . .?

Justin
Yeah, you might have mentioned it

Kathy
Sorry, do I sound insane?

Justin
Don't be, I'm the same

Kathy *and* **Justin**
It's OK to be a little strange

Kathy *begins to explore – picking up a knife.*

Kathy
Oh wow, an actual cartilage knife!

Justin
You know what all the tools are for?

Kathy
I've been reading Reddit threads about them all my life
– ooh

She picks up a saw.

Kathy *and* **Justin**
A metacarpal saw!

Justin
Y'know, most people freak out when they come down here

Kathy
Maybe they haven't found what I have found here
'Cause what I'm about to say might sound morbid
Even thinking it's wrong
But . . .
The moment I walked through that door it's
The first time in my life I've felt there was somewhere . . .

A chorus of **Morgue Technicians** *sing along – all very Disney.*

Morgue Technicians
Somewhere . . .

Kathy
. . . I belonged!

Morgue Technicians
Somewhere she belongs!

Kathy
These bodies are frozen

Morgue Technicians
She belongs!

Kathy
But my soul's on fire

Justin
Oh you can tell me that you want to leave

Kathy
But then I'd be a liar

Morgue Technicians
Tell the truth!

Kathy *and* **Justin**
I've found a place here

Morgue Technicians
There's the proof!

Kathy *and* **Justin**
And I can't deny it

Kathy
Here I am surrounded by death and I've . . .
Never felt so alive

Justin   Here, take a look at this – evidence found at Felicia Taylor's crime scene.

Kathy   Oh my God!

He holds up a beermat.

(*Nonplussed.*) A beermat?

Justin   Yeah, but look at the back – it's got a ten digit number written on it.

Kathy   Oh wow, a cypher! Could it be a cypher? Is that a cypher?!

Justin   We thought that. Turns out it's just the confirmation code for her train tickets.

Kathy   Oh. Yeah, that makes sense too.

Justin   Here, have you ever thought about working somewhere like this yourself?

Kathy   What? Me?

Justin   I could talk to my old forensics course leader in Manchester. Put in a word.

Kathy That'd be amazing . . . but . . . I couldn't. I've got the podcast with Stella, and the library, and my mum wants me to be a teacher, so . . .

Justin They all sound like things other people want. What about you?

Beat. She considers this.

Kathy
Everyone always asked that
How do you answer when you don't know?
I just did what they told me to
'Cause I was terrified of telling anyone no
Tried to meet expectations
But I crashed and burned and then came running home
Couldn't explain that the problem was
That I never had any dreams of my own
And who'd have thought that in a mortuary
I'd find the way that my life ought to be
Sign me up for my first autopsy 'cause I've . . .

Morgue Technicians
I've . . .

Kathy
I've never felt . . .

Morgue Technicians
Never felt . . .

Kathy
Never felt so alive!

We shift outside – to **Stella** *and* **Erica**. **Stella** *is writing a post.*

Stella
Sorry followers, it's so unfair
We've got some intel we'd love to share
It sucks but it's under police embargo
We wanna podcast about it, but we literally can't though
Sad face angry face FML

Erica   It's so stupid – can't they see it's a huge link to –

Stella   The Hull Decapitator. That's what we said!

Erica   But what if he strikes again? The murder gang need to know! *Ruthless92*, *Disrespectress*, *ForensicSteve*!

Stella   You know all our listeners?

Erica   Of course I do. Surely there's some way to let them know.

Listeners *appear and sing seductively.*

Listeners
  Stella tell us

Stella
  I mean they're basically just my friends?

Erica
  Exactly!

Listeners
  Stella tell us

Stella
  I could just slide it into their DMs?

Erica
  I think you should!

Listeners
  Stella tell us

Erica
  They've got to have it!

Listeners
  Stella tell us!

Stella
  This could make us massive!

Listeners
  STELLA TELL US!

Both
Who cares what the police said!

Stella
Ah, fuck it! THE KILLER SENT US FELICIA TAYLOR'S HEAD!

Message alerts start pinging as people start to share! The **Listeners** *become the chorus alongside the* **Morgue Technicians**.

Listeners
OMFG! WTF! GTFO! STFU!
SHE BELONGS!

The scenes overlap: **Kathy** *and* **Justin** *re-enter, still overjoyed in the morgue, as* **Stella** *and* **Erica** *delight at the news becoming public.*

Kathy
These bodies are frozen

Morgue Technicians
SHE BELONGS

Kathy
But my soul's on fire

Stella
Christ alive, will you look at this

Stella *and* **Erica**
It's going viral!

Listeners
Likey like

Kathy
'Cause I've found my place here

Listeners
Sharey share

Stella
And the view count's rising!

Kathy
   Here I am surrounded by death
   But I've never felt so

Stella
   I've never felt so

Erica *and* **Justin**
   I've never felt so

All
   Never felt so alive!

Kathy
   So alive. So alive. So alive. So alive . . .

The song shrinks back and **Justin** *and* **Kathy** *meet in the middle –
close to each other – a sweet moment . . . will they kiss?*

Kathy   Would you like to go for a drink sometime?

Justin   Of course . . . but I'm gay.

Kathy   Oh! Right, yeah, no, I meant just as friends.

The song ends – **Kathy** *and* **Justin** *awkwardly separate as* **Stella**
and **Erica** *enter.*

Stella   Kathy! We've gone viral!

Kathy   What?

Stella   I posted about the head – I know, I know, I wasn't
supposed to – but it got retweeted by *Lorraine Kelly* and now
we've got 10,000 new subscribers!

Kathy   You shared it without telling me?! How could you
do that? We weren't supposed to do that!

Stella   Kathy . . . *Lorraine Kelly*.

Erica   It's all over True Crime Tiktok! You guys are
celebrities! We should get a selfie. It can go on the wall next
to Felicia's.

Stella   Yes! Hang on, you took a selfie with a dead body?

Erica   No. She was here last week. Did Justin not say?

Justin   Oh, yeah, sorry, bit of a sensitive topic – she was here to review new DNA tests that had been commissioned – on the Hull Decapitator . . . that eliminated Billy Fingers as a suspect.

Kathy   Hang on, you're telling me that the week before Felicia Taylor died, she discovered the man she accused of being the Hull Decapitator was not in fact the Hull Decapitator.

Stella   Do you not think you should have led with that?

Kathy   Wait!

A haunting refrain begins as **Kathy** *sings in excitement . . .*

That's why she was here!

Stella
The secret project

Kathy
She was reinvestigating the murders
And what if she found the actual killer
But before she could tell the world, he killed her!

Stella   What happened to Little Miss Stick to the Facts!

Kathy
I know but if what I'm thinking tracks
And we can work out what she knew
Find her final steps and retrace them

Stella   We won't just solve her murder . . .

Both
But the whole bloody investigation

Patricia (*off*)   Very impressive, girls.

The True Crime famous vamp begins again as **Patricia** *enters – * **Felicia***'s sister. Just as ruthless and narcissistic, but less flamboyant, seductively all business.*

Kathy *and* **Stella**   Felicia Taylor?

Patricia *laughs.*

Patricia   Wrong!

> I see your thinking
> Kathy, Stella
> But Felicia's dead and gone
> I'm her sister
> My name's Patricia
> I know you're busy but this shouldn't take long

Stella   Felicia was your sister.

Kathy   I'm so sorry. For your loss.

Patricia   Yes, tragic. But she would have been thrilled. Her book sales have SKYROCKETED! Although the same can't be said for the prospects of our podcast network – hence why I'm here.

> I've been listening to your podcast
> And what I've heard, well – j'adore!
> A true crime themed crime
> Solved in real time
> That's the sort of concept people can't ignore

Stella   You mean there could be a spot for us on the network?

Patricia   Oh, you're thinking too small.

> When Felicia died we were left without our flagship show
> But I think you girls could fill that gap
> There could be books, tours, a Netflix documentary
> Telling the tale of the murder of the century
> And one last true crime accoutrement

A headline slot at UK Murder Con!

Kathy   Murder Con?

Stella   THE Murder Con?

Patricia   The one and only.

You wanna be
True crime famous
Well, I can make it happen for you – one catch
Find out where the blame lies
Then I'll make your true crime dreams come true
Just solve my sister's killing
And then I would be willing
To lift you both up out of the second string

And make you the face of the whole fucking thing.

She answers a call as she exits.

Hi Paul, yes I've seen the front cover – that's a very attractive corpse!

The Kathy and Stella Murder Podcast refrain begins again –
Kathy *and* **Stella** *record an episode – this time with a new
excitement. They're on a roll and their listeners are loving it.*

Both

Hello people
All our brand new listeners
Nice to have you with us
Welcome to our global smash-hit show!
Get ready for some juicy details
As we discuss the latest clues
On this week's episode
of . . .
Kathy and Stella's Murder Podcast
We're gonna crack the case

Listeners

We love you!

Both

Kathy and Stella's Murder Podcast
To learn whodunnit, watch this space!

Stella
We're checking the details and recapping 'em

Kathy
Tracking locations and Google-mapping 'em

Both
Bringing this perp to justice at last
On the world's new favourite murder podcast

The listeners excitedly follow every detail as **Kathy** *and* **Stella** *explain.*

Stella   Oh my God, murder gang – we've been knocking on doors all around Hull – turns out there were witnesses the police never even interviewed.

Kathy   And we've also been going through old newspapers in the archives – we've discovered details even Felicia didn't know about!

Stella   So we've made a profile based on all of this.

Kathy   We're looking for a man – tall, dark hair, left handed. Probably a psychopath.

Stella   So if you know anyone with a history of arson and/or animal torture in the Beverley area, do let us know. But till next time . . .

Both
See you next murder!

Listeners
See you next murder, see you next murder
See you next murder . . .

They stop the recording and celebrate their success as the song segues into a bright Muppety number – 'Everyone's On Our Wavelength'.

Both
Who'd have thought that we could do this
Everyone had us written off
Just some geeky true crime losers

Who couldn't chew what they'd bitten off
Turns out we've made subscribers – of a world who
ostracised us
We used to be outsiders – now everyone's on our
wavelength

Listeners
Wavelength, wavelength, everyone's on their wavelength

Both
And no one else believed in us
But look what we're achieving 'cause
The thing that made us weirdos
Has turned us into true crime heroes

Vanessa *and* **Frankie** *enter – again, in parallel scenes – catching*
Kathy *and* **Stella** *as they pass.*

Vanessa   Kathryn, Maureen from church just said she saw
you on the YouTube . . .

Frankie   Hey, a customer last night said you plugged the
bar on the podcast . . .

Kathy   Oh yeah, we were doing a livestream to raise
awareness about the case.

Stella   Got some new listeners, making a bit of cash,
thought I'd spread the love.

Frankie   Right, well – feel free to backpay the last three
years of rent while you're at it.

Stella   I'm not doing *that* well.

Vanessa   You know . . . I listened to an episode. I haven't
slept in a week. But . . .

Frankie   Just so you know . . .

Vanessa   I'm proud of you.

Frankie   I wish mum could have heard it.

More **Listeners** *enter –* **Patricia** *too. She watches as their show grows and grows.*

Listeners
Everyone's on their wavelength
Everyone's on their wavelength
Everyone's on their –
Everyone's on their –
Everyone's on their wavelength

Kathy *and* **Stella** *part to continue the investigation.*

Listeners
Who'd have thought that they could do this

Kathy
Gotta follow up on all these leads

Vanessa *and* **Frankie**
Who'd have thought that we'd approve of it

Stella
Gotta check our social media feeds

Listeners
Now they've found their vocation
In a homicide investigation . . .
Maybe it's just fate that suddenly –

Kathy *and* **Stella**
Everyone's on our wavelength!

Listeners
Wavelength, wavelength, everyone's on their wavelength

Vanessa *and* **Frankie**
But one thing that's becoming clear
This could be their whole career
How it came to be, we've no idea!
BUT . . .
They might know what they're doing here!

Vanessa *and* **Frankie** *part,* **Kathy** *exits, leaving* **Stella** *alone onstage as the next song begins – quiet, lilting lullaby – 'The Approval of Strangers'.*

Stella *stares at her phone – she can't look away.*

Stella
  I can't stop reading what they're saying about me on the
  internet
  My phone keeps buzzing, people saying they love me and
  I'm here for it
  They're saying
  Stella!
  God, she's so funny
  Stella!
  She makes the darkest day sunny
  And I know that I shouldn't get overexcited . . .
  But how can I not when it feels so right!
  Stella!
  We're so obsessed with her show
  We're all just killing time until the next episode!
  We think she's so fucking cool
  We wish we could go back in time and make friends with
  her on the first day of school

Stella *gets lost in the adoration – like she's appearing in a concert all of her own.*

  I'm getting the
  Approval of strangers
  The approval of lots of strangers
  Lifting me higher with all their tweeting
  It's everything I didn't know I needed.
  From this point on I can't see any danger
  In linking all my self esteem . . .
  To the approval of strangers

As **Stella** *scrolls,* **Tweeters** *appear around her, whispering sweet nothings in her ear.*

Tweeter 1   OMG, Stella is iconic.

Tweeter 2   I literally have her laugh as my ringtone.

Tweeter 3   She's a goddess.

Tweeters
She is everything!

Stella
And every misstep was just steering me nearer to here
All regrets disappear now it's clear
I've been given a chance and I'm not going to waste it
My fate's in my hands, I'll do whatever it takes
So if this is the me they all want me to be
Then that's exactly what I'm going to do
And when the world's seen just how me I can be
. . . even I might end up liking her too

Erica *approaches* **Stella**.

Erica   Stella, it's Erica! I need to give you something. I found it in lost property – it's Felicia Taylor's dictaphone. She must have left it in the morgue the day she died.

Stella   Oh my God – that's amazing!

Erica   I know I should give it to the police – but I think you should have it.

Erica *gives her the dictaphone*.

If there are any clues – they'll be on there.

Stella   I don't know what to say.

Erica   You really are making a difference.

Erica *hugs* **Stella** *and leaves as, elsewhere,* **Justin** *enters and finds* **Kathy**.

Justin   Kathy, I did what you asked – I spoke to my old forensics course leader in Manchester. She said applications for this year have closed . . . but she'd make an exception – for you.

Kathy   Oh wow, that's incredible . . . it's just . . .
Manchester. I'd have to leave Stella. Hull. The podcast.

Justin   . . . if it's not what you want . . . I could tell her no?

Kathy   No wait . . . I've been reading about it online all
week . . .

Beat.

Tell her *yes*.

Justin *leaves to do just that.* **Kathy** *and* **Stella***, each alone, begin
to sing – overlapping with each other.*

Kathy
 Even if I'm rejected, I've spent too long feeling terrified

Stella
 I finally feel accepted for the person that I am inside

Kathy
 I'm done conforming to the crowd, or any dumb societal
 norms, it's OK to be a little strange

Stella
 They don't care if I'm too loud or sometimes unreliable,
 none of them are asking me to change

= Kathy
 Yes, it's kind of scary but the only thing I'm wary of is how
 to break it to my friend I might be leaving

= Stella
 And I've done it with the friend who never stopped
 believing

Their lyrics stop overlapping.

 How could I ever've done this alone?

Kathy
 How do I tell her I've got to go . . .?

Stella
The approval of strangers

Kathy
Gotta choose myself

Stella
The approval of strangers

Kathy
Can't live for somebody else

Stella
They've fallen in love with me and my bestie

Kathy
I've finally found my purpose

Both
This is destiny
From this point on my life will totally change – 'cause
I've finally found . . . myself

Stella
In the approval of strangers

Kathy
I can't stop reading 'bout the life I could be leading . . . on
the internet

The song ends. **Felicia Taylor** *re-enters – recording a message onto
her dictaphone – but as* **Kathy** *and* **Stella** *play it, it is interrupted
by fuzzes.*

Felicia
So the investig – (*Fuzz.*) a thrilling chase – a race against
– (*Fuzz.*)

Kathy   What's going on?

Stella *holds up the dictaphone.*

Stella   The files are all corrupted. She must have spilt
something on it.

Kathy   Can you not clean it up?

Stella   I'm trying, aren't I? I'm just running it through a repair – here, how about now?

Felicia
Saffron, garlic – (*Fuzz.*) truffle oil –
(*Fuzz.*) tooth paste – (*Fuzz.*) kitchen roll

Stella   That's just her shopping list.

Kathy   Skip forward, there must be something on here.

Stella   OK. Final one. This was recorded the day she died. Come on . . .

The sound of static, they both sigh.

Oh, for fuck s –

But then . . .

Felicia
. . . solved the case . . . (*Fuzz.*) found my man . . . (*Fuzz.*)

Kathy   What did she just say?

Stella   Oh my God!

Felicia
. . . the suspect is the source . . . (*Fuzz.*)

Stella   What does that mean?

Felicia
. . . Got the perpetrator . . . (*Fuzz.*)

Stella   Write this down!

Felicia
. . . George . . . (*Fuzz.*)

Kathy   George!

Felicia
. . . Duke . . . (*Fuzz.*)

Kathy   Duke!

Felicia
   . . . Dave S . . . (*Fuzz.*)

Kathy   Davis!

Felicia
   . . . is the Hull Decapitator! (*Fuzz.*)

Felicia *exits* – **Kathy** *and* **Stella** *are left with this revelation.*

Stella   Oh my God. George Duke Davis! George Duke Davis! Have we got anything on a George Duke Davis?

Kathy   No, but there's one here on Facebook – says he lives in Hornsea. We can research more on the way!

Stella   Yes! (*Suddenly.*) Hang on. I thought you said there was only a forty-five minute window on her final day we couldn't account for.

Kathy   Yeah?

Stella   So how's she getting from Hull to Hornsea and back in forty-five minutes during rush hour?

Kathy   Well – maybe she was planning to go after the signing?

Stella   No, she was booked on a train back to London. You saw the reference on that beermat.

Kathy   I know, I did . . .

Something clicks.

. . . *wait!* It was written *on a beermat*!

Stella   Yeah, that's what I just said!

Kathy   No! Where on our timeline did it say she went to a pub? Unless . . . here – look!

She whips out the beermat from the morgue.

The logo – the George pub, here in Beverley!

Stella Aw, that's the one we went to in sixth form – back when it was called . . . *the Duke!*

Kathy The one where you threw up in Stephanie Garner's handbag!

Stella Kathy, I've told you before – I was wrongfully accused!

Kathy That doesn't matter! The Duke! George Duke! It's not a person, it's a pub. And remember who it was run by? That weird old guy!

Stella Yeah, Dave something. Dave . . . Davis? Dave S! She's not saying Davis – she's saying Dave S!

Kathy Dave S. D.S.

Both *D.C.S.!*

Kathy The code-name Felicia used for her anonymous source – the one who tipped her off about Billy Fingers.

Stella (*gasp*)
 The suspect is the source

Kathy Of course. What better way to throw Felicia off the trail than by accusing somebody else of your own crimes!

Kathy *starts Googling on her phone.*

Stella Until DNA tests proved that Billy Fingers was innocent. We've gotta find this guy's last name!

Kathy I already have.

She holds up her phone.

Slatter. David Clive Slatter. D.C.S.

Stella *looks like she's seen a ghost – she goes to grabs 'Heads Will Roll'. An ominously funky vamp begins for 'If I Did It'.*

Kathy What?

Stella

I've seen that name before
Right here! Page ninety-four.
He was an officer on the investigation
That's how he must have faked the information
That stitched up Billy Fingers

Kathy

Wait – I'm gonna Google him – oh wow
You'll wanna take a look at this – right now

It says here he was fired from the police for gross misconduct.

Stella   Fired from the police, he must have been *really* bad.

Kathy

Look, here, I've found a picture
Tall, dark hair, just like that description!

Stella

Jesus fucking Christ

Both

The profile fits exactly

Kathy

He's got a history of assault and battery
It says he was apprehended
And sent to prison
In '97

Stella

Isn't that . . .

Both

The year the killings ended . . .
Are you thinking what I'm thinking
'Cause I think if what I'm thinking is true
We both know what we have to do!

Kathy *and* **Stella** *arrive at his pub, in makeshift disguises, ready to investigate. A sign reads 'KARAOKE – EVERY THURSDAY – 8 till late (11pm)'.*

Stella   Have you got your undercover name?

Kathy   Yep – and d'you remember the codeword to make a swift exit?

Both   Lentil soup.

Stella   OK. Let's do this.

They step into **Slatter***'s pub – he's behind the bar – lascivious, pleased with himself, with undertones of menace . . . VERY SUSPICIOUS.*

Stella   Mr Slatter? Mr David Clive Slatter?

Slatter   Who wants to know?

Stella   My name is Ellen Ripley and this is my associate . . .

Kathy   Buffy Summers.

Stella   We've come to talk to you about a woman who was murdered . . . Felicia Taylor.

Slatter   Oh yes.

  I've been expecting you
  The true crime famous two
  Come to prod me with your probing questions
  My life's an open book, so be my guest and
  Ask what you want to ask me?

Stella   Did you murder / her?

Kathy   / Did she come and see you? The day she died.

Slatter
  She came to me, that's right
  Said new facts had come to light
  Then she hit me with her accusations
  A bunch of truly heinous allegations
  That I was the one who did those murders around here
  long ago

Which is ridiculous . . . 'cause if I did

   . . . No one ever would know – 'cause . . .

He grabs a microphone and performs as if doing karaoke.

  'Cause
  I would never be caught – if I did it
  My case would never see court – if I did it
  I'd toy with them for sport – if I did it
  There'd be no clues at all
  Someone else could take the fall
  No one would prosecute me
  'Cause I'd murder anyone who accused me!

Kathy   Right . . . well, we better be going!

Stella   No, no! We still have some questions actually . . .

  Where were you on the night of her death?
  At 10pm

Kathy
  Or thereabouts?

Slatter
  That's the night I went off my meds
  So I can't account for my whereabouts

Kathy
  Did you torture animals when you were small?

Slatter
  How'd you know about that – which one of them talked?!

Stella
  Are you able to feel empathy?

Slatter
  Look, I know why you've got it in for me!
  You think that I did it, c'mon now, admit it
  And hey, you may be right
  But if it was me, then I guarantee
  It'd never come to light

. . .
'Cause

The **Patrons** *in the pub sing along, as* **Kathy** *surreptitiously records him.*

Slatter
I would never be found

Patrons
If he did it!

Slatter
I would never go down

Patrons
If he did it!

Slatter
I would terrorise the town

Patrons
If he did it!

Slatter
I'd be the greatest killer in history
My identity would be a mystery
There'd be no resolution to this story!

Slatter *hits some top notes as the song climaxes.*

If I did it
If I did it
If I did it
I would never be caught if I did it

As the song ends, we shift to **Kathy** *and* **Stella**, *playing their recording of* **Slatter** *to* **Sue**.

Sue   He sounds like a man with a serious mental illness.

Stella   But he's basically confessing!

Kathy   We've got it all on tape – you have to trust us!

Sue   Why? So you can make my life even more difficult?
Y'know, I remember when Felicia Taylor first came to town
'investigating'. She pointed the finger at the first misfit who
got thrown her way. She didn't care if he was guilty – just
that it made a good story. But this isn't a story – it's real life!
If you want to help . . . *stay out of it*.

Sue *leaves*.

Stella   Right . . . *THAT'S IT!*

Back in the garage, **Stella** *goes to her laptop. A new underscore
begins – urgent, intense and fiery – 'Guilty as Sin'.*

Kathy   What are you doing!

Stella   What do you think I'm doing? I'm uploading the
interview.

Kathy   What? But she just said –

Stella   I heard what she said Kathy . . .

    I don't give two shits anymore
    I'm done with playing nice
    She might not see it, but I'm sure
    He did it, and you know I'm right?

Kathy
    Well, yeah, of course, I don't disagree
    But we need to approach this rationally
    We're not just vigilantes

Stella
    Let's nail this creep without her

Kathy
    We need to formulate a plan please

Stella
    No, we need to get an episode out there!

Kathy   Stella!

    That's exactly what she said not to do

Stella

And exactly what we've got to do . . .
C'mon Kathy, what's that quote?

Both

Evil triumphs when good people do nothing

Stella

We have to make a stand

Kathy

There must be some other way

Stella

It's only you and me who can stop him!

Both

By taking the law into our own hands . . .
'Cause we've no other choice
Y'know we've come too far
If we play by the rules then we'd only be letting him win

Stella

There's no time to lose

Kathy

Because we know it's the truth

Both

So let's give 'em the proof
That he's guilty as sin

Kathy *and* **Stella** *sing into their podcast microphone.*

= Stella

He's guilty
Everybody will see
Listeners, listen to this
He's guilty guilty guilty guilty

= Kathy

Let's take back control
Can't just do what we're told

Gotta let the world
That he's guil –

Kathy *recoils, thinking better of it.*

Kathy   Well, technically we don't have any actual proof, do we?

Stella   What? Kathy, we got it all on tape!

Kathy   I know . . .

And it's certainly incriminating
But there's still room for doubt

Stella
He could be out there decapitating!
He's the killer – so let's call him out!

Kathy
We don't have evidence to show that
He never actually said it

Stella
But our listeners don't need to know that
With a crafty little edit

As **Stella** *plays the recording,* **Slatter** *re-enters and sings the lines.*

Slatter
If I did it
If I did it

Stella *makes a cut in the recording –* **Slatter** *becomes more monstrous as he says the new words.*

Slatter
I did it
I DID IT!

Slatter *exits –* **Kathy** *is horrified by this.*

Kathy
That's total fabrication

Stella

No, it's a bit of artful curation

Kathy

It's immoral and unethical

Stella

But it's justified when together we'll
Solve the murder of Felicia Taylor
And the case of the Hull Decapitator
Right now, before it's too late

Kathy

Stella stop, you've got to wait

Stella

There's no other choice

Kathy

No, we're going too far

= Stella

We can't play by the rules when we know that he's guilty as
sin

= Kathy

We can't break all the rules, even though he seems guilty
as sin

Stella

You've just gotta trust this

Kathy

Can we please just discuss this!

Stella

No, we need to bring him to justice!
'Cause after that then nothing stands between us

Kathy

Why don't you ever listen?

Stella

And living the kind of life we've always dreamed of

Kathy
It's not just your decision

Stella
Kathy don't you see

Kathy
Wait, before we –

Stella
This is our chance to be

Kathy
Don't ignore me!

Stella
Part of the story –

Kathy   I don't know if I want that anymore!

Beat. This hangs in the air.

Stella   What?

Kathy   There's a course . . . to be a forensic technician. At Manchester University. Justin gave me the application form. I was going to tell you . . .

Beat.

Stella   . . . you're leaving?

Kathy   No! No . . . I don't know . . . and even if I do, it's not that far . . .

Stella   *It's the other side of the Pennines*! What about me? What about the show? You're just going to throw that all away?

Beat.

Kathy (*defeated*)   I . . . I don't know.

Beat.

Stella   Right, well . . . Fine. *Fine!*

Stella, *outraged, goes to her laptop.*

> You might not wanna do the right thing
> But I'm not just gonna quit!

Kathy

> Don't you dare upload that episode

Stella

> Too late . . . I already did

Stella *hits upload.*

Slatter*'s 'I Did It's echo as* **Kathy** *and* **Stella***'s* **Listeners** *appear around the stage, their phones dinging and lighting up. People are listening to the episode . . . and a mob is forming.*

Slatter

> I did it
> I did it
> I did it
> I did it
> I did it
> I did it
> I did it
> I did it

Characters we've met emerge from the melee before being reabsorbed – it all gets very 'One Day More'.

Justin *and* **Erica**

> Oh my God, have you heard – they've gone and found whodunnit!

Mob

> EVIL WILL BE PUNISHED!

Justin *and* **Erica**

> He's still out there walking free, that can't be allowed

Sue   What the fuck have they done now?!

Mob

> GUILTY!

Kathy

Why couldn't you listen to me, what you've done is
misleading

Stella

I thought you were leaving

Patricia

Girls! I want you to remember where you are
'Cause today is the day that you both became stars!

Voices overlap as the mob overpowers the song. **Kathy** *and* **Stella**
watch this all play out on their phones.

= Patricia

Got to bring this to an end
We can't let him reoffend
He must be apprehended
Before he kills again

= Mob A

Evil triumphs when good people do nothing
Evil triumphs when good people do nothing
Evil triumphs
Evil triumphs
Evil
Evil
Evil . . .

= Mob B

We're the only ones who can stop him
We're the only ones who can stop him
Got to stop him
Stop him
Stop him
Stop him

= Kathy *and* **Stella**

Oh my God
Oh my God

Oh my God
Oh my God

The online mob hold their phones up like torches – ready to burn **Slatter***'s pub down to the ground.*

Mob
'Cause you can tell from his voice
That he's the killer for sure
There's no fucking way he's not TOTALLY GUILTY AS SIN
Got to make him pay
GUILTY
There's no other way
GUILTY
Need to hunt him down today
'Cause he's guilty as . . .

Kathy*'s phone rings – the mob suddenly disperses.*

Kathy   It's a withheld number.

Kathy *answers on speakerphone.*

Hello? Hello?

A strangled, digitally distorted voice is heard – **The Killer**.

The Killer (*V/O*)   Funny. That's exactly what Felicia Taylor said – before I killed her.

Stella   What? Who is this please?

The Killer (*V/O*)   Oh you know the answer to that . . . *don't you?*

Kathy and Stella's Murder Podcast
Consider me a fan
So thrilled you cracked the case at last
Shame you blamed the wrong man
Never mind there's more fun to come
I'll see you both at Murder Con
If you're wondering who I am, you'll never guess . . .

The various characters we've met appear to **Kathy** *and* **Stella** *– * **Patricia**, **Slatter**, **Justin**, **Erica**, **Sue** . . . *all suspects.*

Patricia, **Slatter**, **Justin**, **Erica**, **Sue**
   For who could ever solve a crime
   Who could ever solve a crime
   Who could ever solve a crime like this???

Kathy *and* **Stella**   Fuck!

Blackout.

End of Act One.

Act Two

Another overture begins – ominous, grand, building and building until . . .

. . . a school bell rings.

Under this, a sweet and music boxy tune begins – this will become 'Read About a Murder' – it's reminiscent of the kind of song you might have sung in school assembly.

A date reads: 2004.

A ten-year-old **Kathy** *runs outside, in a school uniform. She sits on a swing. She takes out an oversized hardback book and starts to read.*

A dinner lady is heard but not seen.

Dinner Lady (*V/O*) Kathy Baxter! Don't just sit there on your own, go and play with the other children!

Kathy I'm just finishing this chapter!

Stella *enters, also ten, also in a school uniform. She drops a Hula Hoops wrapper.*

Dinner Lady (*V/O*) Stella Carmichael! Pick up that litter – I saw you drop it!

Stella What? It's not even mine! So unfair!

She picks up the Hula Hoops wrapper . . . and immediately drops it again.

Stella *sees* **Kathy**. *They glance at each other then look away bashfully.*

Stella *sidles up to her.*

Stella Can I come and sit here?

Kathy Yeah.

Stella *sits on the swing next to her.*

Stella   I was going to play netball with the other girls but I don't want to now 'cause they said I run like a tree and that's not fair 'cause I don't, I'm just dyspraxic. I'm Stella Carmichael, from 5K.

Kathy   I know. You were a sunflower in the harvest festival assembly. I'm Kathy Baxter. From 5W. I was a watermelon. I'm just going to read now.

Kathy *goes back to her book –* **Stella** *peers over, trying to see what it is.*

Stella
  What's that you're reading?

Kathy
  Just a book

Stella
  Where's it from? Can I have a look?

Kathy
  I found it in the library
  I got my nan to get it out for me
  My mum says that it is 'unsuitable'
  If she finds out, I'll get into trouble
  So I read it here at school instead

Stella   What's it about?

Kathy *holds it up – it's a copy of 'Heads Will Roll' by Felicia Taylor.*

Kathy
  A man in Hull who chopped off people's HEADS

Stella   Oh my God . . .

  That sounds like the greatest book that's ever been written in the world EVER . . .

Kathy
  Do you think, maybe, you might wanna read it . . .

Both

  . . . together?

We step up the tempo and flash forward – they're in class, swapping true crime books at their desks. A sign reads: 2006.

Stella

  This one's about a psycho – who did it with his victim's corpse

Kathy

  This one's about a farmer – who fed his family to his horse

Stella

  This one's about an arsonist – who burnt nine people at the stake

Kathy

  This one is Sweet Valley High . . . oh, I got this one by mistake
  Look, a teacher who kidnapped kids and turned them into sex slaves

Stella

  How about a killer clown who buried women in shallow graves?

Kathy

  This one's got a serial rapist who shaved off all his victim's hair

Stella

  This one's about a paedophile!

A teacher is heard but not seen.

Teacher (*V/O*)

  Hey, what are you doing back there?

Kathy *and* **Stella**   Nothing!

  Yes, we know we have to hide it from the world
  'Cause these are things meant just for grown ups
  Scary things our parents think that ten-year-old girls

Aren't supposed to know
But . . .
D'you wanna read about a murder with me
A gory story that we're not supposed to see
They're scary but so exciting
Kinda funny but also frightening
When I read about murder with you
The world seems bigger than it used to
It's kinda strange, I can't explain, or put it into words but,
I know you feel the same, so I'll see you next murder . . .

As the scene ends, we travel forward four years.

We're at a bus stop – a date reads: 2010.

Kathy and **Stella** *re-enter – still in school uniform, but more teenagery, grungey, with elements of their present day outfits over the top.*

Stella   Who the fuck does Hannah Long even think she is calling us morbid?! What? 'Cause we wrote ONE blogpost about her being kidnapped and murdered – now we're not allowed to go to one of her house parties ever again?!

Kathy   It was supposed to be educational. The whole bit about escaping restraints in an abduction situation – that blog post could save her life!

Stella   Exactly! Plus they should all be being nice to me. My mum's in hospital.

Kathy   I know . . . But hey – I don't care about any stupid party. Not when we've got the new Channel 5 documentary about the Hull Decapitator to watch . . .

Kathy *produces a VHS tape.*

Stella   Oh my God! Is that the one with the interview with the woman whose brother owned the cocker spaniel who found the first body? I thought we missed it!

Kathy I taped the repeat. So don't you worry about Hannah Long or any of those other idiots. We've got true crime to keep us company . . .

None of them are smart enough to understand
They're all obsessed with boys and drinking

Stella
And fingering!

Kathy
Urgh!

Both
They may laugh, but we'll be laughing last
When they're stuffed in the boot of a car by a psychopath
with no idea what to do . . .

They savour this thought perhaps a little too much.

They're gonna wish they watched shows about murder with us
Can't they see there is so much to discuss?
They can keep their popularity
All I need is to know you're here with me
Just talking 'bout about murder together
That's why we'll be friends forever!
Whatever comes our way
However our lives change
This is the way our friendship's always gonna stay . . .

One more time jump: 2016.

An old sofa appears. **Kathy** *re-enters in a duvet. She sits – depressed, alone.*

Until . . . **Stella** *enters. She has two mugs of tea.*

Stella Hey, stranger . . . your mum said you were home from uni . . . Thought I'd say hi . . .

She offers **Kathy** *a mug but it's not taken.*

Kathy   Yeah . . . I told her I didn't really want to see anyone, so . . .

Stella   Yeah, I know, but . . . I've just started listening to the Murdergeddon Podcast, I think you'd really like it . . .

Stella *starts to sing again – the same melody as when they were kids on swings.*

> I know you wanna be left alone
> But I've got to play you this episode
> About a guy who hid inside a woman's dishwasher . . .

Kathy   No. Stella . . .

The music cuts out.

I've fucked everything up. I just . . . I fucked it all up.

Beat.

Stella   That's not true. I mean, yeah, you dropped out. At least you went. All I've done is work at Claire's Accessories. And I got fired for giving a ten-year-old a navel piercing. Sometimes life just gets a bit fucked. Doesn't mean it's your fault. And hey, you're better off than this dishwasher woman. That guy killed her with a colander. Imagine being killed by a colander.

A long beat.

Kathy   Actually – it was a salad spinner.

Stella   Ah, so you have listened to it!

Kathy   . . . maybe.

Kathy *can't help but smile. They share a moment.* **Stella** *offers her a mug again and this time she accepts it.*

Stella   Y'know, I actually think *we'd* be really good at doing a podcast. 'Cause no one knows more about true crime than you and obviously I'm hilarious . . . I mean, no one'll listen . . . but what do you think, ey?

Music begins again as **Stella** *tries to coax* **Kathy** *out of her funk.*

Stella

Do you wanna talk about murder with me?

A gory story of –

Kathy *joins in.*

Both

– a life we're glad not to lead

Kathy

Are you sure that we could do it on our own?

Stella

Mate, it's easy – we'll record it on our phones

And if you talk about murder with me

It might be just the thing you need . . .

I know it's dumb

Kathy

. . . It could be fun.

And I'd be chief researcher?

Stella   Duh!

Kathy

Well, I've got no other plans

Both

So I'll see you next murder . . .

They clink mugs as the song ends.

Then suddenly . . .

We hear the sound of a tape being fast forwarded. **Slatter***'s 'I Did It's echo underneath as we hear snippets from Act One:* **Stella** *singing 'Guilty as sin . . .',* **Kathy** *singing 'No, we're going too far . . .',* **Stella** *exclaiming 'It's the other side of the Pennines!' and finally The Killer whispering 'I'll see you both at Murder Con . . .'*

Then suddenly we are transported to a new place – and a new song begins – 'Murder Con'. It's mysterious, dramatic, sexy. Greatest Showman on steroids.

People flood the stage – **True Crime Fans**.

In spotlight, **Patricia**.

Patricia
Welcome to the UK's premiere true crime adventure

True Crime Fans
At Murder Con

Patricia
A weekend of exclusive events

True Crime Fans
At the Birmingham Convention Centre

Patricia
Get in line, 'cause you won't wanna miss it

True Crime Fans
Whoa!

Patricia
Book online, just 400 pounds a ticket

True Crime Fans
Ooooooooooh – wow!

Patricia
So much to see so check your schedule
Reserve a seat though 'cause they'll all get full

True Crime Fans
Your favourite authors are signing autographs

Patricia
For an additional fee

True Crime Fans
Lectures by criminologists explaining trends on graphs

Patricia
Statistically

True Crime Fans
Tonight!

Patricia
Documentaries premiering

True Crime Fans
And then!

Patricia
Evening drinks at the Premier Inn

Patricia *and* **True Crime Fans**
Just a half hour queue and then we are in . . .

True Crime Fans
We are in – we are finally in!
WOO!

Patricia *and* **True Crime Fans**
Welcome to Murder Con!
Where the fans of true crime come to connect
So come get your murder on!
'Cause it's loads of fun and surprisingly respectful
Somewhere you can be yourself where no one else will
judge you
Just take a step inside
We promise you will find
This weekend all about death will be the best weekend . . .
The best weekend . . .
The best weekend . . .
. . . of your life!

Kathy *and* **Stella** *enter from opposite directions –* **Kathy** *fights through the crowd to get to her.*

Kathy
Stella!
Thank God! We need to talk

Stella
  Oh, so you decided to come

Kathy
  How else could I find you – you've not been home
  You've been ghosting me since posting that episode
  And don't say your phone is broken

I can see the blue ticks on WhatsApp.

Stella   Yeah, well, maybe I had nothing to say to you.

A group of **Fans** *run by screaming,* **Justin** *and* **Erica** *emerge from the hubbub.*

Justin   Kathy, Stella, over here! It's us!

Erica   Justin and Erica!

Justin
  We've got tickets for your Q and A at one

Erica
  And t-shirts with your actual faces on

Justin
  I'd say I can't believe it but I absolutely do

Erica
  Now everyone loves you, just like I do

Justin
  Look around you're total stars

Erica
  And we've told everyone that you're friends of ours

Justin
  You caught the decapitator
  And ever since the day that David Slatter's pub was
  firebombed and he was taken into police custody for his
  own protection . . .
  The world's felt a little bit safer

Kathy   But it's not!

Beat. They all look at her.

Kathy
Well, technically he's not been charged

Erica
But we all heard him say 'I did it'

Stella
Yeah, he did say that, those words exactly
(*To* **Kathy**.) And no one can say he didn't!

Justin
Ooh! Look at the time – we've got to run!
There's a reenactment of a hostage situation

Justin *and* **Erica**
We've got to get our blindfolds on.
God we love Murder Con!

Justin *and* **Erica** *chest bump and exit.*

Kathy   What are you doing? You know that's not true!

Stella   Yeah, well, you'd know all about *lies*, wouldn't you?

Patricia *enters and makes a beeline for them.*

Patricia   Girls! There you are. I've been looking
everywhere for my two true crime queens!

Follow me – no shirking – you two
Have a busy day of networking to do

Kathy   Actually we need a moment to talk

Stella   Er, no we don't!

Patricia   Fab! Let's walk

Your last episode has gone down a treat
And there's VIPs to meet and greet
Yes, the True Crime glitterati is here
But they're all supporting artists this year
The top billing on the marquee is clear

The **True Crime Fans** *return, serenading them serenely.*

> 'Cause you're the ones, they've come to see
> They all want Kathy and Stella

True Crime Fans
> Oh my God, it's true!

Patricia
> It's a golden opportunity
> You've got a killer story to sell

True Crime Fans
> We love what you do!

Patricia
> You're the girls from Hull
> Who made a stand

True Crime Fans
> Make a stand!

Patricia
> Don't miss this chance
> To build your brand

True Crime Fans
> Build your brand!

Patricia
> Strike now before that chance is gone

True Crime Fans
> Don't miss this chance!

Patricia
> 'Cause you're the stars of Murder Coooon

The chorus of **Fans** *separate the girls.* **Kathy** *attempts to make her through them towards* **Stella***.*

Patricia *and* **True Crime Fans**
> Welcome to Murder Con!

Kathy   Stella!

Patricia *and* **True Crime Fans**
Where your dreamiest true crime dreams come true
So come get your murder on!

Kathy   Excuse me.

Patricia *and* **True Crime Fans**
If you play your cards right you'll make a fortune
Somewhere you can meet your heroes and maybe you'll
become one

Kathy   Let me through!

Patricia *and* **True Crime Fans**
So leave your past behind

Kathy   Sorry.

Patricia *and* **True Crime Fans**
And just enjoy the ride

Kathy   Oy!

Kathy *almost reaches* **Stella** . . . *but* **Patricia** *comes between them as the song climaxes.*

Patricia *and* **True Crime Fans**
This weekend all about death is gonna change your life so

True Crime Fans
Step into Murder Con!

Patricia
They know your name 'cause

True Crime Fans
Viva la Murder Con!

Patricia
You're true crime famous

True Crime Fans
Got a fervour for murder
We'll deter ya no further
Welcome to Murder Con!

They let off confetti cannons for a big glitzy production number end!

A new underscore begins immediately – tense, paranoid, tricksy –
'You Can't Trust Anyone'. As the chaos disperses, **Kathy** *finally gets*
to **Stella** *who is talking to a fan . . .* **Kathy** *grabs her and pulls her*
away.

Stella   Oy! I was talking to someone actually!

Kathy   What are you doing? You're acting like everything's
fine?!

Stella   It is fine! You heard her. We're stars. So maybe try
enjoying that, yeah?

Kathy   No, Stella, what about the phone call – we need to
tell someone!

Stella   Kathy, I already told you – that phone call was a
hoax! Some prank caller. It wasn't even real. David Slatter
was the Hull Decapitator and we caught him. Deal with it.

Kathy   *But that's not true*! I think we accused the wrong man.

Stella (*hushed*)   Can you keep your voice down? Are you
trying to get us cancelled?

Kathy   I'm *trying* to get through to you! Everyone here is in
danger. And it wasn't just the phone call. Please, for once in
your life can you just listen to me?!

   I went back through all of our research
   Looking for details we might have missed
   I did a deep dive on David Slatter
   And it turns out . . . the killer's profile didn't actually fit*!*

Stella   What? Yeah, it did!

Kathy   No!

   He didn't live in Hull when the killing's started

Stella
   Maybe he commuted

Kathy

He's not left handed or the right size shoe

Stella

So, he's ambidextrous and he wore big boots
None of this proves anything
The guy confessed on tape!

Kathy   No he didn't!

You edited him saying I did it!
Our evidence against him was fake!

We have no idea who murdered Felicia. We never did. Our only suspect is whoever made that phone call!

And you heard what he said
He'd see us both at Murder Con
Right now he could be somewhere near
The real killer. He's here . . .

Kathy *gestures out into the crowd as we transition into a shadowy, dream-like state . . . characters we've met appear and disappear – all now suspicious.*

Look around, it could be anyone
How do we know he's not a face in the crowd?
How can we just let them carry on?
We've gotta say we got it wrong – now!

Stella

This is just your paranoia

Kathy

No, he's right there and he's toying with us

Stella

You sound insane right now!

Kathy

What if he kills again?!

Stella

Calm down!

Kathy
      You can't trust anyone
      We can't trust anyone
      Trust me
      From this moment on
      You can't trust anyone
      Just me
      'Cause everything we thought we knew was wrong
      Every fact we thought was true – a con
      And every lead that we pursued was a dead end all along
      So you can't trust anyone

Suddenly, flashbulbs, fans screaming and people shouting their names – they're shocked back into Murder Con as the voice of **The Killer** *is broadcast over the tannoy.*

Voice of the Killer (*V/O*)   I'M WATCHING YOU MURDER CON – I'LL SEE YOU ALL . . .

Kathy *and* **Stella** *look around – suddenly seeing* **Patricia**, *using an electronic voice-changer to talk into the tannoy. She takes it away from her mouth.*

Patricia   . . . at the true crime auction. Where you can find murderabilia – such as this nifty voice changer . . .

She speaks into the voice-changer again.

Patricia (*in the voice of the killer*)   IT'S TO DIE FOR . . .

Stella *urgently pulls* **Kathy** *away from any fans.*

Stella (*hushed*)   Alright Miss Marple!

      Let's just pretend you're right – you're not
      Then what exactly are we supposed to do?
      You want to tell all this to everyone?
      Hmm. Take a moment to think that through!

Have you forgotten where we are?

We go back into the dream state. The **True Crime Fans** *appear – all coloured by* **Stella**'*s view of them – they're all adoring fans.*

Look around
They're all here to see us
Don't you get it? We're the headline act
So go ahead, tell them we fucked up!
How d'you think they'll all react?

The **True Crime Fans** *morph from adoring to suspicious and back as* **Kathy** *and* **Stella** *argue.*

Kathy
Everyone's a suspect here!

Stella
No! Everybody loves us here!

Kathy
One wrong move – we'll wind up dead!

Stella
All of this is in your head!

You can't tell anyone
We can't tell anyone

True Crime Fans *(joyous)*
Murder Con!

Stella
Even if we're wrong
You can't tell anyone

True Crime Fans *(suspicious)*
It could be anyone!

Kathy
All of them deserve to know the truth!

Stella
All you've got is theories – where's the proof?

Kathy *and* **Stella** *sing over each other as the* **True Crime Fans** *continue to swirl around them.*

Kathy
No . . .

Stella
We caught the killer – we deserve this

Kathy
We got it wrong

Stella
I get it's big and you get nervous

Kathy
It's all a con!

Stella
But I swear there's no one here who wants to hurt us . . .

Kathy
Look around, it could be anyone

True Crime Fans
YOU CAN'T TRUST ANYONE!

Suddenly the **True Crime Fans** *disperse,* **Patricia** *enters, on the phone, hushed, urgent and suspicious. She doesn't see* **Kathy** *and* **Stella** *and they overhear it all.*

Patricia
Darling, you can't tell anyone
But before Felicia's death
The podcast network was almost done
We were out of our depth
But this case has turned our fortunes around
These girls have picked us up off the ground.
If I'd only known how much it would have helped

(*Malevolent.*) Well . . . I might have just gone and killed
Felicia myself . . .

Kathy *and* **Stella** *take this in – both their brains are working quickly . . .*

This is the final straw for **Kathy** *and* **Stella** *knows it.*

They turn to each other.

Stella
OK, look I admit – that sounded suspicious

Kathy
Oh my God, don't you get – just how serious this is?

Stella
Oh, I get it, you're just spiralling

Kathy
We've gotta tell the truth

Stella
Keep breathing!

Kathy
No! We can't keep on denying this!

Stella
What do you care – you're leaving!
And you might wanna fuck this up for yourself
But I won't let fuck it up for me too!

Kathy
I'm not fucking it up – you caused this mess
By editing that interview

Stella
I was doing it for the greater good!

Kathy
No, you were doing it for you!
And I told you not to but you didn't listen
All our lives you never listened
We were supposed to be a team

Stella   Then why were you walking out on me?!

Beat.

The underscore continues but they're no longer singing – everything they've not said to each other bubbles to the surface.

You were walking out. On me. On us. On everything we've
done together. Off to Manchester, bye bye, Stella.

Kathy   I wasn't walking out, I just . . . I found something
that *I* wanted for a change.

Stella   Yeah, by taking the one thing that's ever gone right
for me in my entire stupid life and throwing it down the
shitter! After everything I've done for you.

Kathy   . . . everything you've done for me?

Stella   Yeah, when you had your big breakdown and came
home – I was there for you Kathy! I've always been there for
you!

Kathy   I was there for you too! But what – does that mean
I'm not allowed to do anything on my own ever?

Stella   . . . Yes!

   Because we're Kathy and Stella – that's who we are
   That's who we've always been
   Look around – it's Murder Con
   This was supposed to be our dream

Kathy
   No, not like this – we got it wrong
   We need to make them all aware
   Stella, please, you know I'm right

Stella   Even if you are – *I don't care!*

The **True Crime Fans** *re-enter and circle them – the world becomes
topsy-turvy, nothing is as it seems.*

True Crime Fans
   Can't trust anyone . . .
   Can't trust anyone . . .

Kathy
   You can't be serious

Stella

    Don't fuck up everything we've worked for

True Crime Fans

    Can't trust anyone . . .

    Can't trust anyone . . .

Kathy

    The killer's here with us.

Stella

    I won't go back to the way things were before

    Trust me – before you go too far!

Kathy

    Trust you?! I don't know who you are!

Stella

    Just think – what you're doing'll ruin us

Kathy

    This is so much bigger than the two of us!

True Crime Fans

    YOU CAN'T TRUST ANYONE!

    YOU CAN'T TRUST ANYONE!

Kathy *tries to get past.*

Kathy   I'm gonna tell them!

Stella   No!

Stella *shoves her back – both are shocked by the physical aggression.*

True Crime Fans

    YOU CAN'T TRUST ANYONE!

    YOU CAN'T TRUST ANYONE!

Stella *takes* **Kathy***'s hands, pleading with her.*

Stella   Kathy, please!

Kathy   Let me go!

Kathy *pushes her hands away. They square up to each other – neither backing down.*

Stella
  If you do this – you and me are done!

Kathy
  If I don't – Felicia's killer's won!

True Crime Fans
  LOOK AROUND – IT COULD BE ANYONE!

Suddenly **Sue** *enters having heard the shouting, she stands between them.*

Sue   What the fuck is going on?!

True Crime Fans
  YOU CAN'T TRUST ANYONE!

The song ends and we immediately shift to later – **Sue** *has* **Kathy** *and* **Stella** *in a backstage area. She is reading from a notepad.*

Sue   OK, let me start from the top . . . you received a phone call from somebody *claiming* to be Felicia Taylor's killer, who said they'd 'see you here at Murder Con' and your top suspect is the victim's sister, who you heard . . . '*saying something suspicious*'.

Kathy   That's right, yes, exactly.

Stella   You had to tell her, didn't you?

Beat.

Sue   Well, I guess my only question is . . . *is this some kind of fucking joke to you?*

The temperature immediately shifts.

Well? I mean, seriously? Anonymous phone calls? Overheard conversations? What is this? Scooby Doo? *A woman's dead.* And by the way, yes, I did think to check her sister's alibi. D'you know why? Because I'm the only person in this room who knows what *they're actually doing*!

Kathy I'm sorry, we didn't . . . I'm sorry.

Stella No, don't apologise! Alright, Sue, Jesus, we were just trying to help!

Sue It's *Detective Inspector Shaw.*

Stella Whatever. Why are you even here?! Haven't you got crimes to solve?

Sue *Oh no, I thought I'd leave that to the two of you!*

Beat – she collects herself, becoming begrudgingly professional again.

If you must know, I'm on a panel. I didn't want to but the superintendent insisted. Also, there's a meet and greet with the sniffer dogs. Which admittedly is very cute. So, if you'll excuse me . . .

She goes to leave.

Kathy Wait! You can't just leave it there. At the very least we now know that David Slatter's innocent!

Beat.

Sue *considers this carefully . . .*

Sue Oh. He's not innocent.

Stella What? Really?! I told you!

Sue No. I mean. He's a nasty piece of work. Always has been. But he didn't kill Felicia Taylor. Till a few weeks ago, he'd never had any contact with her.

Stella Yeah, he had. He was her anonymous source. D.C.S. He's the reason she accused Billy Fingers of being the Hull Decapitator.

Sue Oh yeah? And how d'you work that out?

Stella Well, we had a recording.

Kathy On a dictaphone.

Stella And she literally said it!

Kathy   Well, not literally.

Stella   No, but she implied it, and . . . and . . . there was a beermat!

Beat.

Sue   Yeah, well, watertight as that all sounds, I can tell you for a fact that David Slatter was not her source.

Stella   How do *you* know?

Beat – is she going to tell them . . .?

Sue   . . . because I was.

Music begins. Haunted, sad – 'Sue's Song'.

D.C.S. Detective Constable Shaw.

Stella   But that means . . .

Kathy   You worked on the original investigation . . .?

Sue   Yeah. I did.

> Y'know I still remember how it feels to be the hero of the story
> I was twenty-one when the case began, and God, I was so sure
> We would catch the villains, save the day, and find the right solution
> 'Cause every case I faced of course'd have a tidy resolution
> And oh, I was gonna make a difference . . .
> You know, I was gonna make a difference . . .

Least that's what I thought.

> They put me on research, and I gladly joined the cause
> In a room so full of evidence, they had to reinforce the floors
> Late nights, early mornings, sifting through the files for leads
> Dead ends, wild goose chases and wasted opportunities
> Mistakes, incompetence, arrogance and ego trips

Stretched resources, underfunding, and a total lack of
leadership
And before you know, it's been a year
You've done your best, but you're no nearer
You blow the whistle – they won't listen
Too late – there's another victim
And there you are at her front door
You're not a hero anymore
'Cause all you feel is fucking numb
As you tell some kid they've lost their mum . . .

Sue *swallows back the emotion – pushing it down again.*

And you think – is this how I make a difference?
Is this really how I'm supposed to make a difference?

We all knew Billy Fingers. He was a drunk, a weirdo, a real
villain. There was never evidence to charge him but . . . I
just knew. So when Felicia turned up . . . I gave her a nudge.
It was only after he died that I began to think maybe I was
wrong. Not that it mattered . . .

'Cause the world moves on . . .
That's it, case closed, they got him
And all the people left behind – well, they just get
forgotten
It all becomes a story – with people clamouring to write it
But the problem with a story – is real life doesn't quite fit
Some cases never get resolved
Some mysteries, they just can't be solved
There's no meaning, there's no justice
All there really is is just us . . .

I'll look into this phone call. But don't get your hopes up.

Kathy   But what do we do now?

Sue   I don't know.

*A round of applause offstage – chants of 'Kathy, Stella!' from
thousands of fans.*

But it sounds like it's time for your Q and A.

Stella   What are we supposed to tell them?

Sue   That's up to you, isn't it?

Sue *slinks away – as she does, an announcement begins and the room shifts around* **Kathy** *and* **Stella** *– transforming into a stage . . .*

Patricia (*V/O*)   True crime fans – it's the moment you've been waiting for! Everyone's favourite podcasting besties – and the women who SOLVED the case of the Hull Decapitator, it's . . .

A bastardised version of the podcast theme plays as **Kathy** *and* **Stella** *appear with microphones to a cacophonous round of applause. This is the last place they want to be.*

Announcer
    Kathy and Stella from the murder podcast
    Welcome them to the stage
    Find out how their case got cracked
    In their murder con exclusive – Q and A

Applause gives way to silence. The hall feels cavernous and empty.

Kathy   Er hi . . .

Her microphone feeds back.

Stella   Yeah . . . hi.

Kathy   Does anyone have any . . . questions . . .

Stella   Wait. Before you say anything. We've got to tell you something . . .

She glances at **Kathy** *who realises what she's going to say.*

Kathy *nods. This is the right thing to do.*

They hold hands.

Stella   The recording . . . of David Slatter . . . It's . . . It's . . .

Suddenly – a voice from the audience!

Horatio (*offstage*)   A LIE!

Horatio Taylor *steps forward – brash, dashing and theatrical – here to put the world to rights.*

I have an announcement – The two women in front of you . . . are frauds!

Everyone gasps – he looks just like . . .

Kathy *and* **Stella**   Felicia Taylor?!

Horatio   Wrong again.

I'm Felicia's *brother*. Horatio Taylor! World famous podcast star, defender of the wrongfully accused and anti-true-crime activist! And I'm here to tell you all that the man they accused is *not guilty!*

Stella   I was just about to say that –

Horatio   ENOUGH FROM YOU!

A spiky underscore plays as **Horatio** *passionately delivers his evidence in patter – like a cross between Harold Hill and Tom Cruise in a 'Few Good Men'.*

If they'd taken just a second for some basic background research
They would have known that David Slatter's not their man
A prolific fantasist, even my sister dismissed him
Hence why she was leaving Hull the evening of her murder

. . . rather than sticking around for further investigations. But that's not all! They doctored evidence. This is a recording of their podcast!

Slatter (*V/O*)
I did it! I did it!

Horatio   And *this* is the recording that the paranoid Slatter made simultaneously!

Slatter (*V/O*)
  If I did it! If I did it!

Horatio   You wrestled the facts into submission and an
innocent man into a cell!

  Luckily for him I was here to restore his reputation
  And expose the fiend who was really behind my sister's
  decapitation
  The person truly responsible for this murderous affair
  A person who is standing – RIGHT . . . THERE!

He points at **Kathy**.

Kathy   Me?

Horatio   No, not you!

Kathy *steps out of the way, revealing* **Justin** *standing behind her.*

Horatio
  RIGHT . . . THERE!

He points at **Justin** *who looks around to see if anyone is standing
behind him. No one is.*

Justin   Me?!

Horatio   Yes, you – Justin Norris. A name only given to you
AFTER your adoption. Before which you were known as
Gareth Fingers! The only son of Billy Fingers, the man
wrongfully accused of murder by Felicia Taylor!

The music builds to a crescendo as he sums up his case.

  That's why you trained in forensics
  So you could clear your father's name
  Only to find on meeting Felicia
  Revenge was more your game
  You tracked her down after seeing her in the morgue –
  clearly believing
  She deserved to die in the style of the killer she accused
  your father of being
  And what's more – I have solid proof

That this man took her life
Look, here! The murder weapon
A cartilage knife . . .

Horatio *produces an evidence bag with a bloody cartilage knife inside.*

Found in his locker. With his finger prints. And Felicia Taylor's BLOOD.

That's right!

He had the means, the motives and the opportunity
To murder my sister by stealth
Justin Norris IS Felicia Taylor's killer
And what exactly do you have to say for yourself?!

Beat.

Justin   . . . I'm adopted?

Horatio   Tell it to the court! I'm making a citizen's arrest. You're not hurting anyone anymore.

A thumping bass line begins, the song is oppressive and explosive – 'The Show is Over'. **Horatio Taylor** *confronts* **Kathy** *and* **Stella***.*

And YOU!

Horatio
You framed a man for murder
Blinded by ambition
You manufactured evidence
By your own admission
It's too late to put things right
That train has left the station
Instead you've bought a one way ticket
To your cancellation!

The two of you are done – the show is over
We never want to hear from you again
And don't try to apologise
'Cause now you've opened up their eyes

> They can see how much you played 'em
> They can see how you betrayed 'em
> So wipe away your crocodile tears and go
> It wasn't nice to know ya
> Your show is over

Horatio Taylor *exits, taking a protesting* **Justin** *with him.*

Justin   Kathy, Stella, I'm innocent! You have to clear my name!

As **Justin** *disappears,* **Erica** *approaches – heartbroken.*

Erica   I trusted you – I thought you wanted the truth! But you're both just liars – lying liars! I can't believe I believed in you!

As **Erica** *leaves,* **Kathy** *addresses the crowd.*

Kathy   OK . . . before anyone, erm, jumps to conclusions . . .

Stella   We did do that – but in our defence . . . we thought he was guilty.

Patricia *returns – scrolling through her phone.*

Patricia   Oh dear girls, it's all gone a bit south, hasn't it?

> Your indiscretions have been plastered
> Over social media
> You're not the face we're looking for
> So I won't be needing ya

Stella
> No, you have to help us!

Kathy
> We're sorry for offending!

Patricia
> Ooh, better check your Twitter feed!
> Your hashtag is already trending!

Patricia *presents her phone to them as they can see. Suddenly, everyone around them becomes the internet – and the internet is angry! A light up sign with #fuckkathyandstella appears, blinding the audience.*

All
FUCK KATHY AND STELLA

The Internet
The two of you are done – your show is over
Your true crime podcasting days are done

Kathy *and* **Stella**
We're really sorry!

The Internet
You fucked up on the internet
Where we never forgive and we never forget

Kathy *and* **Stella**
No, we promise we'll do better!

The Internet
Well – we're not gonna let ya!
We thought that you were EVERYTHING – but it turns
out you're the WORST!
Blocked and unsubscribe!
You're gonna wish you were NEVER A THING – 'cause
now the bubble's BURST!
You better stay offline!
So go – and don't come back for closure
The show is over . . .

The Internet *parts to reveal* **Doomscroller** *one more time.*

Doomscroller
Eat cock and die you fucking lesbians!

Kathy *scrolls through tweets as* **Stella** *frantically writes a note on her phone.*

Kathy   Shit! Shit shit shit! (*Noticing* **Stella**.) What are you doing?

Stella   Writing an apology – we can get this back – we just need to tell a redemption story!

Kathy   No! No more stories – that's what got us into this!

If you hadn't lied about what he said, this never would have happened!

Stella
If you hadn't lied about leaving me, I never would have had to!

Kathy
Why d'you think I didn't say anything – when I knew you'd react like this!

Stella
Don't turn this round – it's not my fault!

Kathy
Oh yeah, of course – it never is!

Stella
Go on then abandon me for your fancy brand new start
– but then
Who'll be there to pick up the pieces when it all falls apart again?

Kathy
Oh, there we are the guilt trip card – why is that not surprising?
You only pick up the pieces for me to distract from the mess your own life's in!

Stella   That's not fair you went too far.

Kathy   Oh yeah, well you went too far first.

Both
You and me are done, this show is over
I never want to talk to you again
From this point on our friendship's through
And by the way – it's not me, it's you!

Stella

Well, sorry I'm not psychic!

Kathy

Yeah, well, I'm not just your sidekick!

Both

I thought if I didn't have you I would die!
Now I wish I'd never known ya . . .
This show is over

Horatio Taylor *enters – podcasting.*

Horatio   And so, dear listeners, that's the end of this appalling tale about the moral bankruptcy of this so-called industry. Opportunists appropriating real world tragedies, not caring about the lives they ruin, as long as they have a product to sell. And you can read more about that in my next book.

As for Kathy and Stella – I hope they're ashamed of
The price that they paid, to be true crime famous . . .

Horatio *exits to reveal* **Kathy** *alone and defeated. She's sat on the floor, back in a blanket – hiding from the world.* **Vanessa** *enters, tentative and terrified of what this means.*

Vanessa   Kathy, sweetheart, please talk to me. I know people are angry – but it's only the internet. No one at church has any idea.

Kathy   Mum – please leave me alone – everything's gone wrong.

Another scene begins in parallel. **Stella** *enters with a bag and clothes, packing to leave – she's running away.* **Frankie** *follows – she's seen* **Stella** *like this before, but it's different this time.*

Frankie   Where do you think you're going?

Stella   I don't know. Anywhere! Somewhere I'm not me. Don't worry – I won't be a burden anymore.

Frankie   . . . If you want me to tell you that you're not a burden I'm not going to lie.

Kathy   Me and Stella had a fight. We're not friends anymore.

Vanessa   Oh, that won't last – not you two.

Stella   The show's dead, Kathy's fucking off – what have I got to stick around for?

Frankie   What and that's it?

Kathy   I should have just done what you said and become a teacher.

Stella   You were right – I was stupid for even trying!

Vanessa   Sweetheart, I never wanted you to become a teacher. I just wanted you to be happy . . . Like she made you.

This hits **Kathy** *– she's not used to hearing her mum speak that way. She looks at her for the first time.*

Frankie   I never thought you were stupid for trying – I thought you were stupid for giving up. Don't give up on her.

This hits **Stella**. *A rare moment of uncomplicated warmth between them. A reprise of 'We're Gonna Wow Felicia Taylor' begins – but this time it's gentle, sweet, beautiful.*

Vanessa
    Darling, I don't want to criticise

Vanessa *and* **Frankie**
    I'm saying this 'cause I care

Frankie
    I don't think you realise

Vanessa *and* **Frankie**
    You're never gonna find a better friend out there

Vanessa
She's the only one who understands you

Frankie
The only one who can actually stand you
The better half you've always needed

Vanessa
I could never help you like she did

Frankie
And I know you've heard all this before

Vanessa
But listening to your show I saw

Frankie
You don't need the approval of strangers to survive

Vanessa *and* **Frankie**
When you're with her . . .

Vanessa
I've never heard you so alive

At last, **Kathy** *and* **Stella** *each have a moment of true connection with their loved one . . . until suddenly, they are each struck by a thought.*

Stella   Hang on!

Kathy   Sorry –

Stella   What was that?

Kathy   What did you say?

Stella   You know I've *heard all this before?!*

Kathy   Listening to our show you *saw?!*

Stella   I've heard it before!

Kathy   A saw!

Kathy *and* **Stella**   Fuck!

Suddenly we're in **Kathy**'s *garage again –* **Kathy** *and* **Stella** *are both on the phone.*

Kathy   Stella?

Stella   Kathy!

Kathy   You've got to come –

Kathy *and* **Stella**   To the garage!

Stella   I'm already there!

They hang up.

Stella   I'm sorry.

Kathy   No, I'm sorry.

Stella   I'm such a fuck up.

Kathy   No – I'm the fuck up!

Stella   No – we don't have time for this!

Kathy   The murder weapon – it must have been planted! Justin wouldn't use a cartilage knife to decapitate someone, he'd use a metacarpal saw!

Stella   Yeah! And the dictaphone! I listened to it again, right? Here!

The ghost of **Felicia** *enters to voice these recordings.*

Felicia
    . . . solved the case (*Fuzz.*) . . . found my man . . .

Stella   And then I downloaded the audio book of 'Heads Will Roll'.

Felicia
    How long till I found my man and solved the case . . .

Felicia *departs.*

Stella   It was fake!

Kathy   That means . . .

Stella   There's only one person who could have done it!

The garage door opens.

We hear the sound of clapping.

And emerging from the darkness, we see . . . **Erica***!*

Erica   Well done! You solved a murder. Too bad you won't live to tell the tale.

She pulls out a machete.

Stella (*through her teeth*)   Lentil soup! Lentil soup!

Kathy   Yeah, I fucking know!

Erica   Yes – I killed Felicia Taylor. I sent you her head! I gave you clues! I guided you through every single step!

Kathy   Wait – you didn't give us clues. Our listeners did.

Erica   What? Ruthless92? Forensic Steve? Disrespectress? All me!

Stella   You've been catfishing us the whole time?

Kathy   Did we have any actual people listening?

Erica   . . . Doomscroller. The eat cock and die you fucking lesbians man. He *was* a random misogynist.

Stella   But Erica, why?

Erica   Why? Because I'm your biggest fan!

A new song begins – 'The One Whodunnit' – sinister, as unhinged as its singer, occasionally switching to perkiness like someone's flipping it with a remote.

I know – big twist – I'm the one whodunnit
And I would've gotten away with it – oh wait, I did!
It was a battle of wits – and guess what? I won it
And neither of you even suspected a thing

I led you on a merry dance as I advanced my plans, you
didn't stand a chance against your number one fan!

You made it too easy, like you were teasing me – but you
couldn't even – see the wood for the trees and . . .

Now we're here!

I can finally lay out the truth for you
And in case it's not clear . . . Hearing it's the last thing you
will ever do!

Quick sidebar:

Erica *suddenly switches into her fangirl mode – the music changes
with her.*

I really can't believe it – total fangirl moment
I'm actually here in your actual home – I mean
Look at the corkboard with all of your clues
The microphones – I knew it – you use Yeti Blues
It's all such a part of you, it's like I'm at the heart of you
Ooh – An old barbecue

Kathy   Sorry!

I think you might be getting distracted

Stella

Can you get back to – what the fuck is going on?

As **Erica** *explains, we see echoes of the previous scenes –* **Felicia**
and her fans reappear, retracing their lines and movements from
True Crime Famous.

Erica

It all started that night with Felicia Taylor
When I heard her disrespect for ya

Felicia   You're nothing special

Erica

I had to make the world appreciate ya
So I decided to sever her neck for ya

Felicia *and her fans exit as* **Sue** *appears, back in the police station.*

Erica

The decapitation

Sue   She was murdered.

Erica

Was an invitation

Sue   Don't get involved.

Sue *exits as* **Slatter** *appears, back in his pub.*

Erica

To solve the crime – that's why I guided you through
I gave you Slatter

Slatter

If I did it!

Erica

On a silver platter

Slatter

I didn't do it!

Erica

Because I knew you'd know exactly what to do!

Slatter *exits and we're back in the garage.* **Erica** *takes out bonds and ties* **Kathy** *and* **Stella** *to their chairs.*

Erica   It's the perfect true crime story – she's the victim. You're the detectives . . . and I'm the killer.

Stella   Wait, if you wanted us to accuse Slatter, why did you phone us to say we had the wrong man?

Kathy   Yeah, and why did you frame Justin?

Stella   I thought you were trying to help us!

Erica   I was. But the plan worked too well . . .

And when everyone loved you you were no longer mine
No one knew I was the reason they'd heard of ya!

But now I've figured out a way to make it all fine!
Spoiler alert: I'm going to murder you!

She approaches them with the machete raised.

Kathy   Wait!

Stella   Yeah, wait! (*To* **Kathy**.) Why?

Kathy   Before you do that . . . don't you want to . . .

Stella   . . . be the guest . . .?

Kathy   . . . on a special final episode of . . .

Both
Kathy and Stella's Murder Podcast?

Beat.

Erica   . . . do you really mean it? Ohmygod. *HASHTAG LIFE GOALS!*

The Murder Podcast theme begins as they hit record.

Kathy
Hello people

Erica   Hello!

Stella
All you lovely listeners

Erica   Love that bit.

Kathy *and* **Stella**
We've got a very special guest

Erica   That's me! Hi!

Kathy *and* **Stella**
This is Erica

Erica *screams in excitement.*

Kathy
She killed Felicia Taylor

Erica   YES I DID!

Stella
And apparently we're next

Kathy
D'you want to tell us why . . .?

Stella   What was it that first attracted you to murdering people?

Erica   You know the answer to that . . . don't you? This way we all get to be part of the same story . . . *forever*. Don't you understand?

Erica *is suddenly in a spotlight – the music shifts to intense 90s Diane Warren power ballad vibes.*

I did it all for you
We were meant to be – you and you and me
You can't tell me it's not true
It's our destiny to be together
I've got it all planned – do you not understand?
That there's no need to be scared
'Cause when I kill you we'll all live forever
WHEN I KILL YOU WE'LL ALL LIVE FOREVER!

The music shifts again – back to sinister – building to a climax.

Stella   I don't know how to say this without being cliched so I'm just gonna say it – YOU'LL NEVER GET AWAY WITH THIS!

Erica   I'm not trying to. If I'm going to be the most famous true crime serial killer of all time . . . I need to get caught. Don't worry. *This* is what you wanted.

'Cause now forever we'll stay
Part of the same story
She'll never hurt you or leave you or lie
There's no other choice 'cause
Since I first heard your voices
If I didn't have you . . . I would die!

Beat.

This line hits **Kathy** *and* **Stella** *hard – they see themselves in her.*

Stella   No. You wouldn't though . . . Erica, life isn't like a story. It's messy and it doesn't fit. I know you think we're special, but if you really love someone . . . you've got to let them go.

Kathy   But it's OK – just because they're not everything to you anymore . . . doesn't mean they're not still the most important person in your entire life. Y'see, Erica . . .

The melody of **Erica***'s power ballad plays again. This time it's gentler, more mature, understated.*

We were just like you
Thought we couldn't live without each other

Stella
But now we know that it's not true
And letting her grow

Both
Doesn't mean I don't love her

Kathy
You've got it all wrong

Stella
The reason we're strong

Both
Is not 'cause we can't be apart

Stella
It's 'cause wherever we go . . .

Kathy
She knows

Erica *leans in to join them.*

Erica   We know . . .

Both
I'll be there in her –

Stella   Now?

Kathy   Now!

Kathy *and* **Stella** *break free from their bonds*

Erica   OH MY GOD, WHAT THE FUCK IS HAPPENING HERE?

Stella   Come on mate! Escaping restraints in an abduction situation?! We've known how to do that since we were fifteen years old!

Kathy   And we weren't actually recording a podcast – it was a livestream!

Stella   Yeah, turns out Doomscroller called the police!

We hear sirens outside – the game is up!

Kathy   Erica, you got true crime all wrong – it's about empathy, community, mutual support – it's not about murdering people!

Stella   Although that last bit should probably go without saying.

Erica *becomes volatile, lashing out with the machete.*

Erica   No! No! We're meant to be . . .

Part of the . . . STOOOOORY!

We suddenly shift into slow motion.

Erica *slashes at* **Kathy**, **Stella** *blocks her way – a slow motion 'nooooo!'*

The machete glances **Stella** *who falls to the floor.*

Kathy *screams a slow motion 'Stelllaaaaaa'.*

She grabs the laptop and swings it upwards, knocking **Erica** *out.*

And suddenly we cut back to normal speed.

Kathy   Oh shit! Stella, Stella! Are you alright?

Kathy *rolls* **Stella** *onto her back.* **Stella** *seems weak – at death's door.*

Stella   Kathy . . . Kathy . . . is it . . . OK?

Kathy   Yes, yes . . . You saved me, you idiot.

Stella   Of course I did.

    If I didn't have you I would . . .

Stella's *head falls back. She slumps to the floor. Dead . . .?*

Kathy *takes this in . . . and lets out a moan of anguish . . .*

. . . until **Stella** *suddenly comes back to life.*

Stella   Sorry, fucking hell! That was a bit of a shock. It's just a flesh wound. I'll walk it off.

Beat. **Kathy** *puts her hand on* **Stella**'s *shoulder.*

Kathy   Y'know, you didn't just save me when you got stabbed by that murderer just now. You saved me by being my friend.

Stella *puts her hand on* **Kathy**'s *affectionately.*

Stella   You and all, mate. And I'm really going to miss you . . . when you're in Manchester.

Kathy   Well, you better invest in some good wifi . . . 'cause we've got a podcast to record.

The Murder Podcast theme starts up one last time but now **Kathy** *and* **Stella** *each have their own microphone – they're no longer recording in the same space.*

Kathy
    Hello people

An unusually long beat.

Stella
All you lovely listeners

Kathy
There's a mo/mentary delay

Stella
/ There's a momentary delay

Both   Oh shit.

Kathy   I'm rebooting.

Stella   We'll edit that out.

*Suddenly we hear **Felicia**'s voice.*

Felicia (*V/O*)   Excuse me, hello, over here . . .

Felicia *steps out, now dressed all in white and silver and sparkles –
a long flowing dress – like Dolly Parton's wildest fever dream. With
a red diamante necklace – like blood drops. She addresses the
audience directly.*

It's me! The ghost of Felicia Taylor
First and only victim of the second Hull Decapitator

No autographs.

Of course you couldn't end the show without me
And arguably it all should have been more about me
So though it's late – I'll just take two secs
To tell you all what happened next

*Characters appear as she talks about them – starting with **Erica**, in
cuffs, brought on by **Sue**.*

Felicia
The police broke down the garage door and put Erica
under arrest

Erica   You'll never keep me down!

Erica *leaves and* **Sue** *approaches* **Kathy** *and* **Stella**.

Felicia
　　Kathy and Stella had solved the case but still Sue wasn't
　　impressed

Sue　　Nothing you've done satisfies to a legal standard.

As **Sue** *leaves,* **Slatter** *enters, looking up, as if in the dock,
addressing a judge.*

Felicia
　　Slatter was freed – but now he's back in prison for GBH

Slatter　　I did do that.

As **Slatter** *exits,* **Justin** *runs to* **Stella**'*s microphone.*

Felicia
　　Justin's name was cleared as well – and now he's Stella's
　　flat mate

Justin　　Are you recording the podcast again? Hi, Kathy!

Justin *leaves and* **Felicia** *addresses* **Kathy** *and* **Stella** – *for a
moment each becomes a little more aware of the audience.*

Felicia
　　Kathy's at university – she's studying forensics

Kathy
　　And in around about twelve years I'll be qualified

Felicia
　　Stella works for her sister – but just to pay the bills

Stella
　　'Cause I've started doing stand up on the side!

And I'm fucking good at it.

Kathy　　She is actually.

Felicia　　Oh, one more thing. What of the Hull Decapitator
I'll let the girls explain . . .

Felicia's *ghost departs. And the fourth wall goes back up. We find* **Kathy** *and* **Stella** *podcasting again – wrapping up the latest episode . . .*

Stella   Well, Murder Gang, that's the end of our story.

Kathy   In conclusion, we've learnt a lot of important lessons about the ethics of true crime investigations.

Stella   And from now on we'll do our best to only *rightfully* accuse people of murder.

Kathy   But a lot of you have emailed in to ask if we ever actually learned who the original serial killer was all those years ago . . .

Stella   Yeah, and the thing is . . .

The innocent twinkle of 'Read About a Murder' returns – but this is a new song. More mature. 'See You Next Murder' . . .

Stella
That's a thread we can't resolve

Kathy
The case as yet remains unsolved
We never learnt the identity

Stella
Maybe it wasn't meant to be

Kathy
Sorry, the end's not satisfying

Stella
But sometimes the world's just . . . horrifying

Both
And yeah, it's kind of hard to not lose hope
But we might have a way to help you cope . . .

Kathy
'Cause you might find comfort in a terrible story

Stella
And if you don't – listen no more

Both
But if you do – then we'll be here for you
If you need tales of crimes
That are all *mostly* true . . .

We'll see you next murder
When the world gets overwhelming
See you next murder
It might help your mental well-being

Kathy
When any hope is hard to see

Stella
And you need a break from the patriarchy

Both
Just tune in and we'll do our best to divert ya

Kathy
When we see you next murder

Kathy
For more morbid fascination

Both
See you next murder

Stella
Y'know, it's fine in moderation

Both
And yes, we know that it's kind of wrong
But as long as we acknowledge that – it's alright to carry
on!

The vocals overlap as the **Listeners** *sing 'Kathy and Stella's Murder Podcast' beneath the following lines.*

Stella
And talk about murder

Kathy

Talk about murder

Both

Talk about murder . . .

Kathy

. . . together, no matter whatever

Both

Wherever we are
Even when we're apart
We'll talk about murder this way
To darken up your brightest day

Kathy

So when every headline seems designed to disturb ya

Listeners

See you next murder

Stella

When you're filled with a sense of existential inertia

Listeners

See you next murder

Both

When it seems like the human race can't decline any
further

We crescendo in a beautiful canon – **Kathy** *and* **Stella** *and their Listeners all singing together. Even Felicia's ghost reappears at the back of the stage – joining in with the fun . . .*

All

We'll see you next murder!
See you next murder!
See you next murder!
See you next murder!
See you next murder!

As the song climaxes, the **Listeners** *and* **Felicia** *depart.*

Kathy *and* **Stella** *are left alone – no longer together, but never truly apart.*

Leaving their microphones, they both address the final line to each other.

Kathy *and* **Stella**
   See you next murder

Blackout.

The End.